easy to make!

Curtains & Blinds

easy to make!
Curtains & Blinds

Expert advice, techniques and tips for window treatments

consultant Wendy Baker

COLLINS & BROWN

First published in the United Kingdom in 2010 by
Collins & Brown
10 Southcombe Street
London W14 0RA

An imprint of Anova Books Company Ltd

Main contributor: Kate Haxell

ISBN 978-1-84340-572-6

A CIP catalogue for this book is available from the British Library.

10 9 8 7 6 5 4 3 2 1

Reproduction by Rival Colour Ltd, UK
Printed and bound by 1010 Printing International, China

This book can be ordered direct from the publisher at www.anovabooks.com

CONTENTS

Introduction

To some people the thought of making their own curtains might seem quite daunting, but as long as you know how to use a sewing machine, can cut straight lines with a pair of scissors and thread a needle you are halfway there.

You don't need to make the whole process complicated, start with a basic pair of unlined curtains for say, a family room or kitchen. When you realise how quick and easy they were to make you can then venture on to the next step by adding lining, and even put a trimming on the hem for the more important rooms.

Try to read the book step by step, as it was designed, without skipping bits that you know, or think you know, because that way you will get a clear picture of how to approach the task without panicking. Let's face it, a pair of curtains are only straight pieces of fabric sewn together – anyone can do that.

Of course, it can get much more complicated the more you add on but again take it in your stride, don't tackle anything too involved until you are more confident. Use a plain fabric to start with and then progress to a printed fabric, as pattern matching can be a bit of a challenge – even for me.

Blinds are very popular and cheaper on the whole, because you don't need as much fabric as you do for curtains. It is very important to make sure that you take accurate measurements. Always use a metal retractable tape measure (metre rule or folding ruler) and then there can be no mistakes. If the blind doesn't fit properly, it will not only look homemade but will also let in the light at the sides or bottom, and is unlikely to hang straight.

Before you start ask yourself a few questions. Do you want curtains? Should they be long or short? Would a blind be better for that particular shape of window? If you choose a big flowery pattern, will it overpower the room? Is the fabric suitable for the curtain or blind or is it too heavy or too thin? There are many decisions to make before you get out the scissors.

Here are a few basic rules, like all rules they can be bent, but you will do well to take them on board to guide you. Choose your pole or tracking to suit the window. If you want to hang the curtains from a pole, make sure it is the right thickness. Thin poles are for thin fabrics and for rooms with low ceilings. Thicker poles are best if the fabric is heavy and the ceilings are high. Always make sure that the pole is wider than the actual window to allow the curtains to clear the frame so that you don't block out the light.

Remember, when choosing the fabric if you pick a thin fabric it will need to be lined, whereas a thicker one may not. Try to steer clear of open-weave fabrics, as they tend to sag out of shape very quickly, and also avoid very stiff fabrics, as they never hang properly.

When you are underway and hopefully enjoying making your own curtains, remember too that in doing so you are saving money as well as creating your own unique soft furnishings.

Wendy Baker

GETTING STARTED

Different types of window

In addition to providing privacy and insulation, curtains or blinds give a room a finishing touch without which it can look rather bleak. Apart from all the fabric possibilities, there are also the different styles of curtain and blind to consider. What you choose will not only depend on your personal taste, but also the style of the room and the type and number of windows in it.

Make sure that the window treatment you choose does not greatly restrict the amount of light that the window lets in to the room, unless blocking light is your aim. Some windows, such as those set into ceilings and those in home offices where light levels need to be controlled, work better with blinds than with curtains.

Shown here are examples of the types of windows commonly found in a home, with advice on what window treatments will suit them.

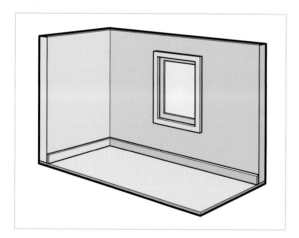

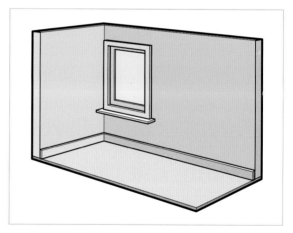

Single window in a wall

This offers the most options for dressing, since you can use virtually anything you like as long as it fits the style of the room. Dramatic statements work well in larger rooms, but keep it simple for smaller spaces.

Window close to an adjacent wall

It is difficult to have a symmetrical treatment because one side of the window has no room to pull back the curtain. Try using a blind or make a feature of the asymmetry and choose a single curtain that pulls back to one side.

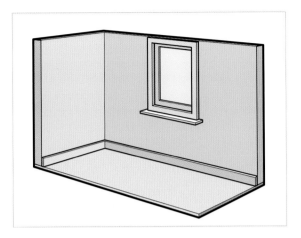

Window close to a ceiling

Here you may have to mount the fixture either on the window frame or on the ceiling. A full length curtain will exaggerate the height of the window when it is closed, so consider either sill length or just below sill length.

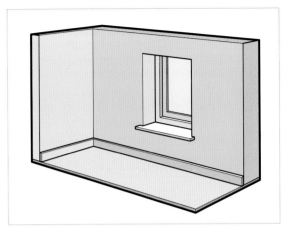

Window in a deep recess

There are two options here: a curtain that runs across the front of the recess or a treatment that sits within the recess. If you choose the latter then it is usually better to have a blind as there will not be enough space to pull back the curtains, resulting in loss of light. As recessed windows tend to restrict light a bit anyway, you probably don't want to loose still more.

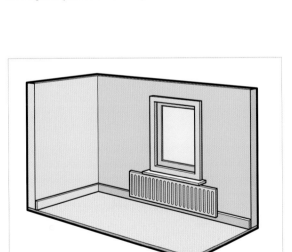

Window with a radiator beneath

Floor-length curtains will block some of the heat from the radiator. One option is decorative full-length dress curtains with a practical blind that comes to the sill for warmth and privacy. The other option is, of course, sill-length curtains, although these are not always an attractive solution.

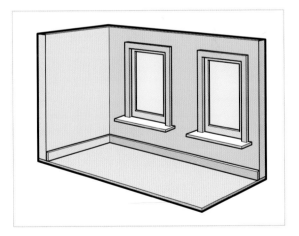

Pairs of identical windows on the same wall

These can be treated as one unit or as two separate windows, depending on how close together they are. If you treat them as separate windows, the treatment for both should be identical or they will have an unbalanced appearance.

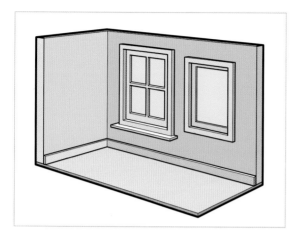

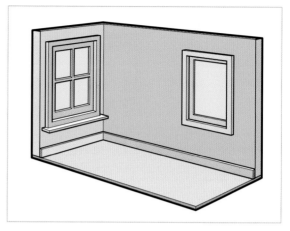

Different windows on the same wall

To tie these windows together visually, work from the height of the taller window and dress both to the same hem level. If the windows are close enough together, and not too different in size, they can be treated as one unit.

Different windows in a room

Where the windows are far apart and dissimilar they can have different treatments. However, it can look odd to have two curtain styles and you may find that two different treatments – for example, a pencil pleat curtain (see page 38) and a Roman blind (see pages 62–65) – are a better choice. Use the same fabric and trimmings for both windows to unite them.

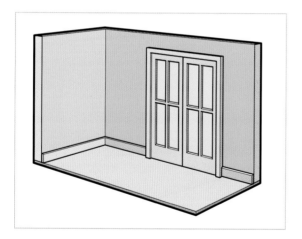

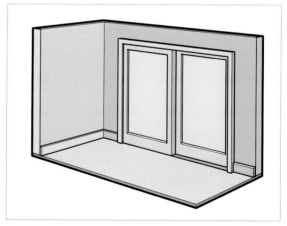

French doors

These will probably need to open for access, so any treatment must bear this in mind. If the doors open outwards, treat them like normal casement windows. If they open inwards, enough stacking space (see page 29) must be allowed on either side so the curtains can be pulled right back out of the way of the doors. A blind could be added to the door for privacy.

Windows or sliding doors taking up all or most of the wall

There may not be much stacking space (see page 29) for curtains and the amount of fabric needed to cover the expanse of glass will make them bulky. Opt for simple sheers (see page 52), or choose dress curtains that do not draw plus blinds for privacy.

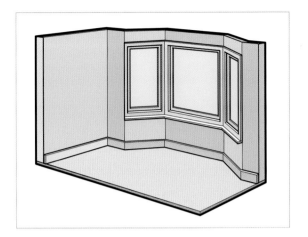

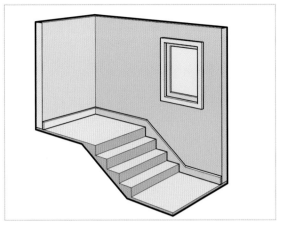

Bay windows

There are three ways of curtaining a bay window. Option one is to have a separate curtain and support for each window, but this can leave gaps at the corners.

Option two is to have one pair of long curtains that open from the middle, which can look more attractive but requires an angled track. Some types of track can be bent on site to fit, otherwise a curved track can be ordered from a supplier. Special poles that bend are also available, but they can be quite expensive.

Option three is to run the curtains across the face of the bay, as long as you don't mind losing the floor space when they are closed.

Alternatively, you can fit each window with a Roman blind (see pages 62–65) or soft pleat blind (see page 66), although again, you risk gaps.

Window on the stairs

Here the main issue is being able to reach the curtain or blind to close it. Make sure the closing mechanism of a blind can be reached easily from the upper level and consider pull cords for a curtain. This type of window usually looks better with a treatment that comes no lower than the sill.

Right: Layers of curtain, even if they are nothing more special than voile sheers (see page 52) and lined curtains (see pages 44–49) can add elegance to a simple room.

Choosing the right window treatment

Whether you choose to dress your windows with curtains or blinds, informal sheers or traditional goblet pleats, tailored Roman blinds or easy-to-use roller blinds, will depend on a variety of factors as well as personal taste. You will almost certainly find that making a decision about one aspect of a treatment affects a completely different aspect of it, so make sure you have considered everything before you come to a final decision.

Style of window

The style of and number of windows that need to be dressed will have some influence on the treatment you choose. Pages 10–13 illustrate some styles and combinations of windows and offer some thoughts on dressing them. It's unlikely that you have exactly the windows illustrated, but some of the principles involved will almost certainly apply to your room.

Above: Roman blinds are a window treatment that work well in almost all styles of room, depending on the fabric you choose.

What window treatments offer

The four elements that curtains or blinds can offer a room are warmth, privacy, darkness and decoration. You may not want or need all four, but that is a decision you must make before you go any further. If you are going to spend time and money dressing your windows, you need to make sure that the treatment you choose is fit for the purpose.

Warmth

Adding interlining to a curtain (see pages 44–49) adds an insulating layer that really will make a difference to the temperature of a room when the curtains are drawn.

A hot part of the world just won't need interlined curtains, although lining will be a good idea to protect the main fabric from the sun. If you live in a climate with cold winters and hot summers, you may want to consider two pairs of curtains; lightweight ones for summer and heavy interlined ones for winter. This also offers the opportunity to give the room a different look across the seasons if you wish.

If the room has central heating provided by radiators, then these are often placed below a window (see page 11). This places restrictions on the window treatment you can use. Full-length curtains will block heat from the radiator when they are drawn, so you need to have either sill-length curtains or a blind. If you are completely wedded to the idea of floor-length curtains, then you should have the radiator moved.

If you are adding interlining, you need a main fabric that is at least medium-weight. If you add the interlining layer to a lightweight curtain fabric, the curtain just won't hang properly.

Privacy

There are usually two forms of privacy to consider; permanent screening for a room such as a bedroom, and screening for a living space that is lit up at night.

The quickest and easiest way to screen a bedroom window is with sheer curtains, but these don't have to be traditional nets. Consider a beautifully patterned lace fabric or embroidered voile that complements the main curtain fabric in either colour or pattern. There's a huge range of sheer fabrics available, so this doesn't have to be a boring option.

When the lights are turned on at night, windows become rather oppressive black panels when viewed from the inside, and from the outside the room is lit up for any passers by. Both are good reasons for having curtains or blinds. If neither warmth nor the restriction of outside light are issues, then you can have whatever style of curtain or blind will suit the room best (see pages 22–25).

Darkness

Usually the rooms that need light blocking out are bedrooms. This is particularly true if you live in a town or city where street lights are on right through the night.

Firstly, make sure that the window treatment you choose completely covers the window, ideally extending beyond the frame a little to completely block light. For this reason, if the window is recessed (see page 11), you shouldn't fit a blind within the recess.

Secondly, consider using a blackout lining, though this does place restrictions on the fabric you choose. As blackout lining tends to the thick and quite stiff, you can't use a lightweight fabric because the curtain just won't hang well.

Decoration

This is always going to be a factor in choosing a window treatment, though its importance will vary. At the very least you are going to want to choose a fabric that suits the rest of the room. At the most, the window treatment is going to be a focal point in the space and so every detail of it needs to be carefully considered.

If the room is already decorated to your satisfaction and you are only dressing the windows, then the fabric and style of treatment will be dictated by other furnishings in the room. If you have left-over paint or scraps of fabric from other soft furnishings, then take samples with you when shopping for curtain fabric. Always get a reasonable-sized sample of your chosen fabric, take it home and look at it in the room, as the light there may be very different from the light in the shop.

If you are completely re-decorating the room, then there are still some factors to take into account when choosing a treatment. Read on for some useful guidelines that will help you decide on the best solution for your windows.

Right: Lace fabric offers privacy, texture and decoration when used to curtain a bedroom window. You'll want fabric curtains, too, to block out light at night.

Aspect

Which direction does the window face? If it's north-facing, then it won't get a great deal of light at the best of times and you need to be careful not to block it in any way. Choose a treatment that can be pulled or raised to completely clear the glass and so let in maximum light.

If you want a Roman or soft pleat blind, this means fixing the mounting board (see pages 64–65) to the wall above the window, high enough for the hem of the blind to clear the top of the window glass when the blind is raised. Don't position it so high that the hem clears the top of the frame, as that will look very odd.

Size of window

If the window is tall, then you absolutely do need floor-length curtains. Short curtains on tall windows just look as though they have shrunk. If the window is tall but the ceiling of the room is relatively low, then you can use a vertically striped fabric to give the illusion of more height.

Wide windows, bay windows, or French or sliding doors (see pages 12–13) require a large amount of fabric, which can add up to a lot of money. They also mean that when the curtains are drawn, the fabric will be very prominent in the room. So choose your fabric especially carefully; you're going to be living with these curtains for some years.

Very small windows need a simple treatment in an unobtrusive fabric or they will look ridiculous. If you choose short curtains then it's usually best not to interline them as they tend to look chunky and stiff.

Colour

Warm colours make things look closer and cosier, while cool colours give a more spacious feel. Enhance favourite aspects of a room by using this visual trick when choosing fabric.

A south-facing, sunny room with a minimalist decorative style will look fabulous with simple curtains in neutral or cool colours. A sitting room with a window facing the chilly north will benefit from curtains in a fabric such as rich orange velvet for delicious visual warmth. So think about what you use the room for and how you want it to feel when you are in it before picking a fabric.

Pattern

This can be a tricky thing to get right and usually the old adage of less is more is very true when it comes to patterned curtains. If the window is very large, then you can get away with bolder patterns, but read through the section on working with pattern (see pages 22–23) before buying.

Fixtures

If you are having curtains then the pole or track you choose can be decorative or purely functional, but it's something you should make a conscious decision about. There are some practical elements, as well as decorative ones, that may affect your decision (see also pages 18–19).

Interlined, full-length curtains can be surprisingly heavy and need a robust support. Flexible plastic track is usually not a good choice, so if you do want track, choose a metal one. However, a pole is usually best for this sort of curtain. Choose one that complements the fabric you are using and ensure that it is firmly fixed to the wall or ceiling.

The style of curtain heading you want to use (see pages 32–41) will also affect the fixture you choose. All the headings shown can be used with a pole, but not all of them work well with a track.

If the top of the window frame is very close to the ceiling, then there may not be room for a pole and you will have to opt for track. However, sometimes you can use special brackets and hang the pole from the ceiling, it just depends on the space available.

Blinds have either a mounting board (see pages 64–65) or a purchased roller blind fitting (see page 68), so you don't have any decorative decisions to make. Just ensure that there is enough space for the fixture and that it can be fixed firmly enough: this is particularly true with roller blinds that can get pulled on rather hard.

Embellishments

Trims can turn a simple fabric into a very luxurious curtain and are a good option if you are working to a budget as you usually don't need that much of them. You can buy an inexpensive, plain-coloured fabric and attach a stunning trim (see pages 72–74) to dress it up.

As well as being practical and holding an open curtain out of the way, tiebacks are another way of making a bit more of a basic drape. You can make your own (see pages 78–79) to complement the curtains, or buy something a bit special, maybe to match the pole (see pages 76–77). You can also get creative and press something more unusual into service, such as the leather belt shown right.

Decorative aesthetic

Once you have made all the practical decisions then personal taste and good judgement come in to play. Do take time to think about your window treatments: if you need urgent privacy, hang a sheet at the window for the time being instead of rushing out and buying the first fabric that catches your eye. Remember that well-made curtains will last for literally years and so you want them to be perfect.

A formal room doesn't have to have a corresponding window treatment, but a formal treatment in an informal room usually doesn't work. A very modern room can take a traditional curtain style if the fabric is carefully chosen, but a contemporary heading, such as eyelets (see page 37), will rarely sit comfortably in a period room.

Buy some interior design magazines, flip through lots of books, take snaps of friends' windows and build up a collection of treatments you admire. There will probably be a unifying theme, and as long as it works visually and practically in your room, that is the treatment you should choose.

Top right: A leather belt is used as a tieback for this curtain, which was made from a thick woollen plaid blanket: an informal tieback for an informal curtain.

Bottom right: The distressed finish on the pole and finial ties in well with the country style of the check fabric and the simple tab-top heading.

Curtain fixtures

Fixtures are the rod, pole or track a curtain hangs from and the hooks and other fittings needed, and there is an impossibly wide range of them available. Do you want concealed or visible, period or contemporary, wood or metal, pull cords or none? To some extent the style of your room and your fabric may influence your choice. There are so many types available that we can show only a few examples here.

Tension rod

This is held in place by tension within a window recess, so there is no need for fixings. It will only hold sheers or very lightweight curtains.

Wooden curtain rod support

This support is screwed to the wall and the wooden curtain pole drops into it. These supports often have decoration that matches the pole's finials.

Spring wire

This is usually attached to the window frame with small hooks and is mainly used for sheers, which are threaded onto the wire.

Wooden curtain rod finial

Finials not only add decoration but also prevent the curtain sliding off the end of the pole.

Pole

Fixtures like this wooden pole are designed to be seen. They come in both wood and metal and in a variety of finishes and styles. This one has a plain finial on the end.

Wooden curtain ring

These rings are threaded onto wooden curtain poles. The curtain is fitted with hooks – plastic or metal – which hook onto the small metal ring.

Metal track

This type of track is not designed to be seen and is purely functional. The side view is discreet and can also be obscured with a pelmet or heading.

Plastic track

Like a metal track this is functional rather than decorative. A plastic track is stable when in place, but bends easily around corners to fit awkward spaces.

Metal curtain rod support

This metal pole support has a screw-in fitting on the front, which can be tightened against the pole to hold it firmly in place.

Small metal cord hook

This type of small metal hook is fixed to the wall at the side of a blind – or sometimes a curtain – to hold the excess pull cord in place.

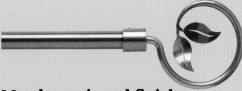

Metal curtain rod finial

There is a wide range of finial designs available, some with matching holdbacks (see pages 76–77) for a really co-ordinated look.

Plastic curtain hooks

Plastic curtain hooks like these slide into the heading tape on curtains, then hook over the loops hanging from plastic track. A similar item is available for metal tracks.

Blind pull

You can buy plain, decorative or whimsical pulls that are threaded onto the end of the blind cord.

Fabrics

There is a huge range of fabrics suitable for making curtains and blinds, and a huge range of prices you can pay. Do remember that your curtains should last many, many years, so it's usually worth buying something you really like and if the fabric is expensive, remember how much you are saving by making the curtains yourself.

As well as personal taste, there are a few practical issues to consider when choosing a fabric. Thick fabric produces bulky curtains, which are not a good option for small windows. Thin fabric will let light through, so it's not the best choice for bedroom curtains. Don't try to line thin fabric with blackout lining as the curtains won't hang well. Sunshine will fade fabrics, so windows with sunny aspects may need voile curtains, or even shutters, to protect the main curtains. The curtain heading you choose will also affect the fabric choice, or vice versa (see pages 32–41).

Wools and wool mixes

There is a multitude of fabrics in this category and most of them are easy to work with and will make up into beautiful curtains. They are not necessarily heavy fabrics and the textures vary from thick, knobbly tweed to herringbone weave to soft, smooth, fine wool. Wool and wool mixes tend to drape well but often do not have a great deal of body. They are ideal for fairly simple curtain styles, and work well for Roman blinds (see pages 62–65).

Be aware that most wool fabrics will need professional cleaning, so might not be suitable for a child's room. Some wool fabrics fray quite badly, in which case you must overlock or zigzag all edges before completing the curtain or blind.

Linen

Flax is a natural fibre that is woven into linen fabric, which is available in a variety of weights. Linen tends to drape very well, so medium to heavier weights can be used with great success to make unlined curtains (see pages 42–43). These weights also work very well with structured heading styles, such as French pleats (see pages 40–41) and goblet pleats (see page 41), both of which are given a relaxed, more casual feel by the nature of the linen itself.

Linen is available in a variety of colours, prints and textures, so there should be an option to suit almost any room. Linen can usually be washed, with caution, though ironing the curtains afterwards can be a major task.

Cotton

As with wool fabrics, there is a wide range of different coloured and patterned cotton fabrics to choose from, and they tend to be inexpensive. Sateen, ticking and chintz are all cotton-based fabrics that work well in curtain making.

Cotton fabric often has a stiff finishing treatment that gives the fabric more body, but this will probably disappear the first time the curtain is laundered, and that could dramatically affect the look of your window treatment. Try laundering a scrap piece of the fabric first and see what happens to it. Measure the scrap before laundering so that you can check if it shrinks.

Velvet

This is one of the most difficult fabrics there is to sew, yet if you can conquer it the resulting curtains or blinds will certainly be marvellous. Do not cut off the selvedges when working with velvet, as it will fray badly. You will need to overlock or zigzag any cut edges.

You can buy printed velvet, and woven stripes are available, but patterns can detract from the luxurious finish of the plain fabric.

Velvet is usually made from cotton, though synthetic and silk velvets are both common. Synthetic velvets often have a crushed finish, which is a little more forgiving for the sewer and the fabric drapes well. Silk velvet is best left for the dressmaker because the price of it makes it extremely expensive for curtains.

Chenille is a cousin of velvet and its weight and more pronounced texture make it a great curtain fabric, especially in period rooms.

You should always line (see pages 44–49) velvet curtains, though heavier velvets do not need the interlining layer.

Silk

Another fabric that is available in a variety of weights and great ranges of colours and patterns, silk can be a less expensive option than you may think. Plain colours work well with the more complex headings such as goblet pleats (see page 41), while printed and embroidered silks make even the plainest style of curtain look special.

Sunshine will actually rot silk, as well as fade the colour, so this isn't a good fabric choice for a sunny aspect: even if you use lining fabric the exposed leading edges of curtains can rot and fray surprisingly quickly.

Silk does make up into fabulous curtains for both period and contemporary rooms. A striped silk made into full curtains with a box pleat (see page 39) heading will look great in a modern formal room, while lightweight, rumpled silk with a simple pleated heading (see page 38) will make elegantly full curtains in a contemporary space.

Voile

This sheer fabric can be bought in many colours and these days you will also find embroidered and sequinned versions for added glamour. Voile provides no warmth and blocks almost no light, but it does offer privacy and decoration.

You can either use voile very full with a casing heading (see page 34) to make billowing curtains that can be dramatic in a bedroom, or you can make simple soft pleat blinds (see pages 66–67) that are very pretty. If you do make blinds, consider getting the fabric treated first so that it is stiffer: your fabric shop or a local blind manufacturer should be able to help with this.

Left: Pin up swatches of fabrics in the room you are making curtains for and see how they look in both the natural daylight and artificial light.

Working with pattern

Using pattern is a great way to add extra interest to a room, but there are so many different types of patterns in different colourways that making a choice can be very difficult. The pattern can be printed or woven, and designs can be contemporary or traditional, geometric or floral, subtle or bold, large or small. Ultimately your choice is personal, but here are some general guidelines that will help you pick your patterns.

Above: The colours are the critical factor with checks; if they are toning the effect will be subtle, but if they contrast the design looks bold, as here. Do bear in mind that a large amount of strong check can overwhelm the rest of a room.

Subtle pattern

Small-scale patterns in toning colours tend to recede visually and are widely used as a background. They make small rooms seem bigger, but tend to disappear in big spaces. In larger rooms, combine them with broader designs.

Bold pattern

Large-scale patterns in strong colours can overwhelm small rooms, but give large rooms a more intimate feel. You can soften bold designs by using plenty of neutrals with them. If you are mixing more than one bold pattern in the same room, make sure they work well with each other by choosing a limited palette of matching colours or related designs.

Neutral and simple patterns

These fabrics can be used as the basis of any interior design scheme. You can then add bolder colours or designs as accent pieces on items that are easy to change when you want a new look. Neutral fabrics can have surface texture or tactile pattern to add interest, so if you are using a selection in one room, make sure they go together (see page 24).

Printed and woven patterns

These fabrics will usually make more of a statement, so they need to be selected and used with some care. Different geometric patterns often work well together, and geometrics can be successfully combined with florals, but too many different florals can look messy. Woven patterns may be double-sided, but printed patterns usually have visible right and wrong sides.

Amount of pattern

Too much pattern in a room will – whether the pattern itself is subtle or bold – look very busy and the effect may be overpowering. It's much better to pick out one or two focal points to use pattern on. Pick out one of the colours in the pattern and use that as the base colour for your scheme to simplify and tie things together.

Pattern on curtains

Curtains have to look good in two very different ways – pulled open and drawn closed. A pattern that looks great gathered up may look too much spread out across a large window, and a pattern that looks lovely when the curtain is drawn may look cramped and confusing when the curtain is pulled open. When you are choosing fabric in a shop, roll out a length of it and stand back to assess the effect. Then gather the length up and stand back again to see how that looks.

Pattern matching

Most patterns will need matching across the seams (see pages 86–87) when you are joining widths for a curtain, though you do not have to match small, over-all pattern in subtle colours. If in doubt, fold the fabric so that two widths lie side-by-side and assess how the pattern looks. Remember that you are going to have these curtains for a while and that skipping the pattern matching may be something you later regret.

Right: A classic floral design is prevented from becoming insipid by its relatively strong colours and large scale. Florals like this need to be used in a way that allows the full effect of the print to be appreciated, so simple curtain styles are best.
This is the same room as that shown opposite, but the change of decor gives it a completely different feel.

Working with texture

Apart from colour and design, the other factor to consider when choosing your fabric is texture. Depending on how it is made and finished, the surface of a fabric can be smooth or highly textured, shiny or matte, flat or with a pile or nap. The surface also affects the colour; two pieces of fabric dyed an identical colour will look very different if one is shiny and the other napped. In addition, shiny fabrics reflect light, making the room appear bigger, while matte fabrics absorb light, making the room feel cosier.

Types of texture

Some fabrics have an inherent, all-over texture that is part of their make up. This can be a woven texture on fabrics such as damask, dupion silk or hand-loomed cotton, or a napped texture on fabrics such as velvet, chenille or corduroy. Other fabrics have an added texture created by embroidery or by fabric manipulation, such as pintucks.

Fabrics with napped or added texture can be quite thick and stiff, so assess how a length drapes and gathers up before buying.

Texture patterns

Patterns can be formed from texture rather than colour, or sometimes from coloured texture. A woven fabric such as damask has a lightly embossed textured pattern, created during the weaving process, that is either self-coloured (the same colour as the background) or a different colour.

Devoré-style fabrics have areas of napped texture forming patterns on an otherwise flat surface. Again, the pattern can be self-coloured or a different colour.

Mixing texture

Generally it is easier to mix textures within a room than to mix patterns, though you do need to exercise a little caution. Too many heavy or patterned textures in a small space can be visually very untidy.

Texture also can affect the way light is absorbed or reflected by the fabric and this can make the colour look quite different. It is best to take fairly large samples home with you and look at them in the room they will feature in.

Mixing texture and pattern

This can be amazingly successful and a good way of incorporating the qualities of both into a room. Match a textured fabric to one of the colours from a patterned fabric and use the texture as an accent.

Curtains in a patterned fabric with cushions in the same fabric and a toning textured fabric will lend a co-ordinated look to a traditional or modern setting.

An informal feel

Some fabrics not traditionally used for curtains will fit perfectly into an informal, contemporary environment. Hessian or burlap, canvas, ticking and rough-weave calico can all be used to make statement curtains that will work best with simple headings such as eyelets (see page 37) or handsewn hooks (see page 37).

Canvas and calico will both dye well in the washing machine, so you can get away from the neutral colour that these fabrics are usually sold in.

Using lace

Usually associated with period or country-style rooms, lace can in fact look good in almost any space. Machine-made lace can be bought in a reasonable range of colours and the designs vary from traditional all-over feather patterns to more modern scattered motifs such as stars and snowflakes.

You can use lace curtains in a similar way to sheers (see page 52), though you will want less fullness to allow you to see the lace pattern. You can also use strip lace to good effect to trim a fabric curtain (see page 73).

Sewing textured fabrics

Woven textures are usually not too difficult to sew, but napped textures can be tricky. Laid right sides facing, one layer can "creep" across the other as you sew it on the machine, resulting in a discrepancy in length at the end of the seam and, if you are particularly unlucky, a badly puckered seam.

There are three ways around this problem. Firstly, a walking foot for the machine that feeds the top layer of fabric through at the same rate that the feed dogs take the bottom layer through: these feet can be expensive. Secondly, you can tack all the seams using alternate long and short stitches to prevent "creeping". Thirdly, you can lay a strip of tissue paper between the layers of fabric and pull it out after sewing.

Experiment with scraps of a fabric to see how badly it "creeps" and try tacking or tissue before buying a walking foot.

When joining fabrics with a pile or nap, make sure the pile runs in the same direction on each piece or the colour will look quite different.

Texture matching

An all-over texture with no discernable pattern – for example, velvet or hessian – will not need matching when widths are joined. A defined texture, whether it is a damask or a napped pattern, will need matching in the same way as a patterned fabric (see pages 86–87). The repeat can be measured in the same way as a pattern repeat (see page 86).

Right: A loose-weave hessian fabric makes for the simplest ever curtain: a length of it is just folded over at the top and attached to a pole with café clips.

CURTAINS

Measuring for curtains

Whatever style of curtain you plan to make, accurate measuring is vital for a professional finish. Use a metre (yard) rule, a folding ruler or a retractable metal tape measure and enlist the help of a friend if the window is large.

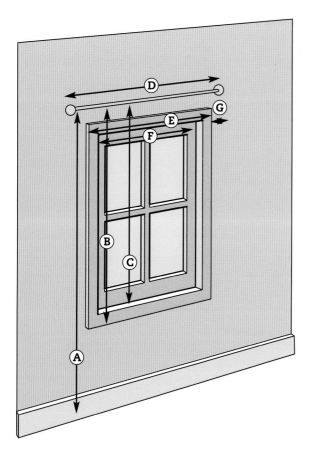

A Bottom of pole, track or rod to floor

B Bottom of pole, track or rod to bottom of window frame

C Bottom of pole, track or rod to sill

D Length of pole, track or rod

E Width of window frame from outside edge to outside edge

F Width of window recess

G Stacking space (also on left-hand side of window)

Glossary of measuring terms

Fabric width – the purchased width of the fabric.

Selvedge – the tightly woven edge of the fabric. This reacts differently to the main fabric to stitching and washing and so should be cut off unless you are working with velvet (see page 20).

Cut width – the width of the fabric after the selvedge has been removed.

Finished width – the full width of the area that the completed curtain is intended to cover, including the stacking space (see opposite).

Widths – multiples of the cut width of the fabric. With the exception of a very small window, you will probably need to join more than one width of fabric to make up a curtain.

Finished drop or drop – the full length of the area that the completed curtain is intended to cover.

Cut drop – the finished drop plus hem, heading and pattern repeat allowances. This is the measurement to cut before assembling the curtain.

Fixture – the mechanism from which a curtain is hung, including tracks, poles and rods. The fixture can be mounted on the wall over the window frame, on the frame or inside the recess depending on the style of the window (see pages 10–13) and style

Curtain fixtures

Before you begin to measure, you need to decide exactly where your curtain will go. If the fixtures are not already in position, you must decide if they are to go above and across the window (D on the diagram), on the window frame (E on the diagram) or within the window recess (F on the diagram). If the latter, then bear in mind that when the curtains are open they will obscure part of the window glass and obstruct some daylight. Recessed windows are best curtained with sheers that are not pulled open (see page 52), or with blinds (see pages 56–69).

It is much better to have the curtain pole, track or rod (see pages 18–19) in place as it's easier to measure from a real fixture than to guess placement. If you can't have the fixture in position, then make a pencil mark where it will be so that you have a point to measure from.

If you are having a pole or rod and rings, then you need to measure from the bottom of the pole or rod, as that is where the top of the curtain will lie. If you are having a track, then measure from the top of the track, as the top of the curtain will cover it.

Stacking space

This is the space either side of the window that the curtains will sit in when they are open (G on the diagram). If you don't leave this space, then the curtains will obscure part of the window when they are pulled open.

The amount of stacking space you need does depend on the style of curtain heading, the thickness of the fabric and whether the curtains are lined and interlined. For lined curtains of medium-weight fabric with a standard pencil pleat heading, allow about 10 per cent of the width of the window (E on the diagram) on either side and that will be plenty. Unlined curtains will need less space and interlined ones, or ones with full headings (such as goblet pleats or French pleats that require a lot of fabric), more space. You can experiment by bunching up a width of your chosen fabric and measuring how much space it occupies.

The curtain fixture needs to be the width of the window plus stacking space. If a pole has finials, then they are added to the length.

Curtain length

The length of the curtains will depend on the style of window (see pages 10–13) and the style of the room. Usually curtains will be floor length, frame length or sill length. If they are to be a different length, then make a light pencil mark on the wall at the hem position (use an ordinary soft eraser to gently remove it later).

Taking measurements

A metre (yard) rule or folding ruler are the ideal tools for measuring a window as they are rigid. If you use a retractable metal tape measure, be sure that it doesn't buckle or twist while you are taking measurements.

To measure finished drop with a rule, hold it flat against the wall next to the window. Slide it up until the top is level with the top of the pole: if the window is tall then ask a friend to stand further back in the room and tell you when the top of the rule is in the right place.

If the curtain hem position is within the length of the rule, then read off the measurement and make a note of it. If the curtain will be longer than the rule, then make a light pencil mark on the wall at the bottom of the rule. Slide the rule down so that the top of it is against the pencil mark. Either read off the measurement at the position of the curtain hem or repeat the process until you do reach the hem position. When you note the total measurement, remember to add up all the lengths of rule that are marked on the wall as well as the final measurement.

If you are using a metal tape measure, then extend a length of it and slide it up the wall until the end is level with the top of the pole. Using one hand to hold the tape flat against the wall, extend the tape with the other hand until you reach the hem position. Be careful that the tape doesn't slip.

To measure finished width if you are using a pole above the window, measure the length of the pole, not including finials, from the inside of one bracket to the inside of the other. If you are using a track, measure from one end of it to the other. If the curtain is within a recess, then just measure the width of that. If you are going to have a pair of curtains (rather than a single one), then divide all three of these measurements in half to get the finished width of one curtain.

Calculating fabric quantity

When you are calculating the amount of fabric you need for your curtains, be sure to allow for pattern repeats, hems, headings and fullness. Follow the formulas given here to work out how much fabric you will need.

Fullness of curtains

Unless you are deliberately making flat panels, curtains require some fullness to look good. The amount will depend on the style of heading you want to use (see pages 32–41) and the type of fabric you have chosen (see pages 20–21).

The standard fullness for medium-weight furnishing fabric is between one-and-a-half and two-and-a-half times the finished width, depending on the look you want and the heading. Sheers and lightweight fabrics will need up to three times finished width, while very thick or heavily patterned fabrics may need only twice the width. This really is a style choice, but remember that flat curtains can look skimpy.

Fabric widths

Furnishing fabrics come in a variety of widths, the most common being 122 cm (48 in) and 137 cm (54 in), though you can get curtain voiles that are 300 cm (120 in) wide.

You need to be a bit cautious about conversions between metric and imperial numbers. Some manufacturers weave in metric and convert to imperial and others vice versa, and the conversions are not always exact. For instance, a fabric woven on a 36 in loom may be labelled as 90 cm, but if measured with a metric rule, it would be a little wider than 90 cm. This rarely matters with curtains as small differences get absorbed, but it can be important for blinds (see pages 56–69).

Cut drop

To the finished drop measurement add 12 cm (5 in) for a hem. Add the amount needed for the heading (see pages 32–41).

If you are using patterned fabric, then check the pattern repeat and add one repeat.

This is your cut drop.

Amount of fabric to buy

Multiply the finished width of the curtain by the required amount of fullness.

Divide this number by the cut width of your fabric.

Round this up to the nearest half number (to allow for seams) to establish how many widths of fabric you will need.

Multiply the cut drop by the number of widths to calculate the required amount of fabric per curtain.

Then round this up to the nearest sensible number.

An example

Finished drop = 230 cm (92 in)
Add 12 cm (5 in) for hem = 242 cm (97 in)
Add 8 cm (3 in) for heading = 250 cm (100 in)
Cut drop is 250 cm (100 in)
NB If you are using patterned fabric, remember to add one pattern repeat to the cut drop.

Width of window = 150 cm (60 in)
Multiply by 2½ times for fullness = 375 cm (150 in)
Fabric width = 122 cm (48 in)
Divide 375 (150) by 122 (48) = 3.073 (3.125)
Round up to nearest half number = 3.5
Multiply 250 cm (100 in) for cut drop by 3.5 = 875 cm (350 in)
Therefore the final amount of fabric = 875 cm (350 in), which is 8.75 m (9.72 yd)
Round up to nearest sensible number – 900 cm (360 in), which is 9 m (10 yd)

Buying the fabric

While you obviously don't want
to waste fabric (especially if it's
expensive), you really don't want to
buy too little to make your curtains
look great. You're going to invest
time in them, so be prepared to
invest some money in them, too.
Work out how much fabric you
need. Do the calculations again to
make sure you've got them right,
then buy that amount and no less.
You can always use any surplus
fabric to make cushion covers to
co-ordinate with your new curtains.

Right: There is a huge array of gorgeous furnishing
fabrics to choose from, so do read the fabric, pattern
and texture pages in this book (see pages 20–25)
before picking one.

Curtain headings

The heading of a curtain is at the top and is attached to the fixture. The pleating or gathering involved in making the heading also serves to pull in the fabric to fit the required finished width. The same fabric made up into curtains with different styles of heading will have very different looks, so choosing a heading is almost as important as choosing the fabric.

Types of heading

Shown on the following pages are basic headings, plus more formal styles that feature hand-made pleats. These are not at all difficult to make, though they do require careful measuring to make them look their best. Here is a summary of the headings illustrated with advice on fabrics and fullness.

Casing (page 34)

This is the simplest type of heading; it is just a tube at the top of the curtain. As the fabric will not very easily slide along the pole, this heading works best for lightweight curtains that do not need to be drawn, such as sheers.

For sheers you can have fullness up to three times the finished width, as a very full sheer curtain can look wonderfully elegant. You need to add four times the diameter of the pole to the finished drop to make this heading.

A casing heading is also ideal for panels made from heavier fabric, though again, these will not draw easily. Panels like this can make stylish banners either side of a large window – a contemporary version of dress curtains that are decorative rather than functional. This can be a great look in a modern but formal room.

Gathered heading (page 34)

One of the plainest headings, this is suitable for many types of curtain. It is made using a narrow heading tape.

Two-and-a-half times finished width in a lightweight fabric will produce full curtains that look fantastic at floor length. In a medium-weight fabric the curtains will hang a little flatter and will work well at a shorter length.

If you want to make quick, unlined curtains (see pages 42–43), this is the heading style to choose.

Handsewn hooks (page 37)

Here the hooks are hand-stitched individually at intervals across the heading. The final curtain will have an understated elegance and hang more or less flat, so you will need very little fullness; one-and-a-half times finished width will be ample.

This is a good heading if you have chosen a heavily patterned fabric and want to show off the design without interrupting it with deep folds.

A flexible style, handsewn hooks work well in both contemporary and period rooms, depending, of course, on the fabric you choose.

Eyelets (page 37)

Another very simple heading that produces a fairly flat curtain needing just one-and-a-half times finished width for fullness.

The eyelets are punched at intervals across the top of the curtain and then threaded with a cord. The pole goes through the loops in the cord.

This is a contemporary, fairly masculine style and can look out of place in a decorative room.

Pencil pleats (page 38)

This is probably the most popular style of curtain heading. It is made using a wide tape that has several cords across it to pull the heading into a series of vertical folds.

You can use this heading with any weight of fabric and two-and-a-half times finished width will usually be ideal. However, if you are using a light-weight fabric and are making full-length curtains, consider using three times finished width for a tightly pleated heading and billowing curtains that look luxurious in a bedroom.

Right: A simple heading can easily be made that bit more special by adding an embellishment, such as these embroidered buttons. Their Scandinavian-style motifs perfectly suit the striped fabric.

Box pleats (page 39)

The simplest of the hand-pleated headings, box pleats can be made to almost any width. The fabric needs to be light to medium in weight and this will affect both the width of the pleats and the finished look.

A lightweight fabric with wide pleats will have a soft, less formal finish, while the same fabric with narrow pleats risks looking skimpy. Narrow pleats in a medium-weight fabric look more tailored, and wide pleats and medium-weight fabric offer a formal effect.

Be cautious of patterned fabrics as dense pleating can cause visual chaos with busy patterns. You will need three times finished width for this heading.

French pleats (page 40)

A very traditional heading style, French pleats can be made by hand or by using a special tape with spaced hooks. The version shown here is the hand-pleated style, as this is easy to make and generally looks better than tape-made pleats.

You can use fabric of any weight and two-and-a-half times finished width will usually be ideal. The photograph above is a variation of French pleats made with just two pleats and embellished with embroidered buttons.

Goblet pleats (page 41)

Formal goblet pleats look best in heavy fabrics and will suit a traditional room. The curtains do need to be floor length to balance the visual weight of this style of heading.

You will need two-and-a-half times finished width: don't be tempted to make the curtains fuller than this as the goblets will either be oddly large or too tightly spaced to look good.

Striped fabrics can look fabulous with goblet pleats, but you need to work out the spacing very carefully so that the stripes appear in the same position in relation to each goblet or the effect can be completely ruined.

Heading tapes and hooks

Heading tapes and hooks should be selected with care; ask the sales consultant for advice if you are not sure. Buy the tape long enough to avoid joins: you need the finished curtain width plus at least 5 cm (2 in) at each end to turn under. Also, match the type of hook to the tape you choose.

Heading tapes have woven guidelines to help you keep your stitching straight, so use them because the lines of stitching do show on the front of the curtain. If your curtain is narrow, you can stitch over the cords at the leading edge and use one set of cords to pull up the tape. If the curtain is wide, it will be quicker to gather from both ends.

After pulling up the cords to get the heading to the required width, knot the cords together near the curtain to hold the gathers in place. Wind the excess cord around your fingers and tuck it into the heading tape close to the end. NEVER cut the cords – you will need to let the heading out again whenever the curtain is laundered.

Many seemingly complex headings can be created easily by using fancy tapes that either have several cords to pull at specific intervals, or have pockets in which to insert special hooks to make the pleats. Be a little cautious, as some of the tapes can be less than successful on some fabrics.

Casing

So simple and quick to make, this heading requires just one line of sewing. The pole or rod slides through the tube of fabric and it's done. Use this heading with an unlined curtain (see pages 42–43) or a sheer curtain (see page 52). You can have up to three times finished width (depending on the fabric) and need to add four times diameter of the pole to the finished drop.

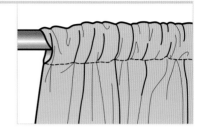

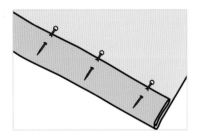

1 Measure the diameter of the pole. Across the curtain top turn under a double hem twice that measurement. Pin and press. Machine stitch along the bottom fold, as close to it as possible, removing the pins as you go. Backstitch at each end to secure the threads.

Right: Curtains with casing headings are great for more than just your windows. Here they are made from ticking and work brilliantly instead of doors on kitchen cupboards.

Gathered heading

A gathered heading is almost as simple as a casing, but the curtains are easier to draw. Gathering tape is available in different widths. Use this heading with an unlined curtain (see pages 42–43), a lined curtain (see pages 44–49) or a sheer curtain (see page 52). You will need up to two-and-a-half times finished width and must add the depth of the heading to the finished drop.

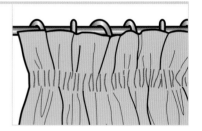

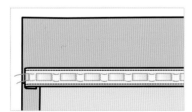

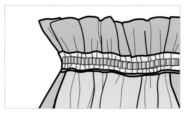

1 Fold over the curtain top the depth of the heading. It should be at least 2.5 cm (1 in); here it is 8 cm (3 in). Pin the gathering tape over the raw edge.

2 Stitch along either edge of the tape. Knot the cords at one end. From the other end, pull up the curtain to the required width. Knot the cords.

This page: A variation on an eyelet heading is to set extra-large eyelets into the curtain and thread these directly onto the pole. You need an even number of eyelets to make the heading symmetrical.

Handsewn hooks

Handsewn hooks work well on café curtains (see pages 54–55), but can also be used on full-length unlined curtains (see pages 42–43) or lined curtains (see pages 44–49). The hooks can be visible (as shown right) or concealed behind the curtain (as in Step 1. You will need one-and-a-half times finished width and must add 5 cm (2 in) to the finished drop.

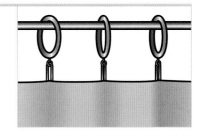

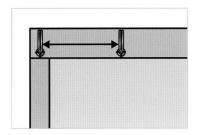

1 Turn under and stitch a double 2.5 cm (1 in) hem across the top of the curtain. Measure the width of the curtain and divide it into equal spaces: the exact space will depend on the width of the curtain, but should not be more than 15 cm (6 in). Mark each

measured point with a pin. Stitch a hook at each mark, either with the end protruding above the top of the curtain or fully concealed behind it.

Eyelets

Metal eyelets in brass, steel or pewter finish are available in good fabric shops. Ensure that the eyelets are large enough for the cord to pass through. Use this heading with an unlined curtain (see pages 42–43), a lined curtain (see pages 44–49) or a sheer curtain (see page 52). You will need one-and-a-half times finished width. The depth of the top hem will depend on the size of the eyelets: the hem must be deep enough for them to sit within it and they should be at least 1.5 cm ($\frac{5}{8}$ in) from the top of the curtain. Add twice the hem depth to the finished drop.

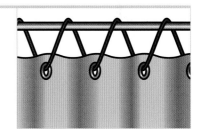

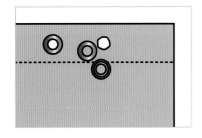

1 Make a double hem of the required depth and divide the top edge of the curtain into equal spaces, as for Handsewn Hooks. The eyelet kit will come with fixing instructions, though you will need a hammer and a hard surface: don't use the dining room table

as hammering the eyelets WILL mark it. Fix the eyelets into the top of the curtain, ensuring that they sit within the hem. Loop the cord evenly through the eyelets and thread the pole through the cord loops.

Pencil pleats

Pencil pleats are thin, evenly-spaced, straight pleats. For tight pleats, as here, you will need three times the finished width, though two-and-a-half times will still create a good effect. The depth of the heading will depend on the tape: add this depth to the finished drop. Use this heading with an unlined curtain (see pages 42–43) or a lined curtain, with or without interlining (see pages 44–49).

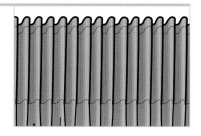

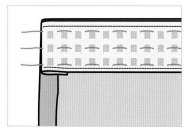

1 At the top of the curtain, fold over a single hem slightly narrower than the width of the heading tape. Position the tape so that it covers the raw edge of the fabric and the upper edge lies just below the top of the curtain. Pin the tape in place across the curtain. Tuck each end of the tape under, but pull the cords free. Stitch the tape to the curtain along the top and bottom edges.

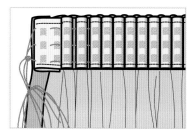

2 Knot the loose cords at one end and pull on the other end to gather up the fabric into even pleats until the curtain is the width required. Spread the pleats across the curtain. Knot the free cords, wind the excess cord around your fingers and tuck it into the tape.

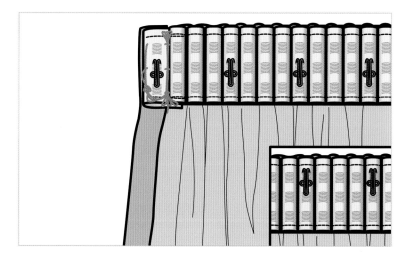

3 Slot the hooks into the tape. There is usually a choice of two or three levels for the hook, depending on whether you are using a track that the heading should cover or a pole that you want to show. Place one hook at each end of the curtain and space the others about 8 cm (3 in) apart.

Box pleats

Box pleats do not need heading tape. They must be set up by hand, but they are simple to do. You can use this heading with an unlined curtain (see pages 42–43) or a lined curtain (see pages 44–49), though you may find that adding interlining will make it too bulky – it depends on the fabric. You will need three times the finished width and should add 2.5 cm (1 in) to the finished drop.

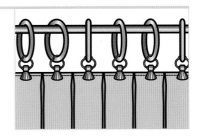

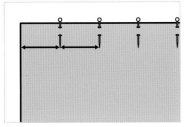

1 Measure and divide the curtain into equal amounts across the top, marked with pins. You need three pins for each pair of pleats, so the total number of pins (not spaces) across the heading should be divisible by three.

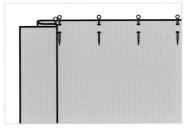

2 Fold the fabric along the line of the first pin and then bring the fold over to meet the second pin.

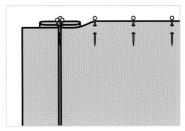

3 Fold the fabric along the line of the third pin and then bring the fold over to meet the second pin. Pin the folds in place about 5 cm (2 in) from the top edge.

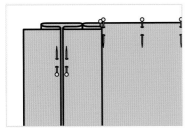

4 Fold at the fourth pin and the sixth pin, and bring the folds to meet at the fifth pin. Continue in this way across the full width of the heading.

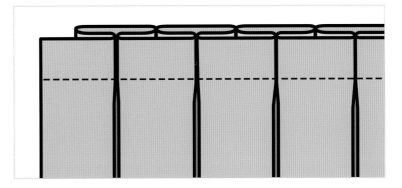

5 Stitch across the top of the curtain about 2.5 cm (1 in) from the top, keeping the pleats square. Remove the pins and press the tops of the pleats. Fold over the top of the curtain and finish on the reverse by making a hem or binding the raw edge. Café clips (as shown, top) or handsewn hooks (see page 37) are good ways of attaching a box-pleated curtain to a pole.

French pleats

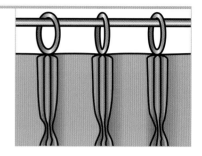

French pleats are also known as pinch pleats. They consist of groups of (usually) three pleats that are pinched together and stitched at the base and fan out at the top, with flat areas between the groups. This style of heading works well with lined and interlined curtains (see pages 44–49). You will need two-and-a-half times the finished width and should add 20 cm (8 in) to the finished drop.

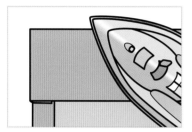

1 Fold over 20 cm (8 in) along the top edge of the curtain to the wrong side to make a deep hem and press. Cut a length of fusible buckram 15 cm (6 in) deep and 15 cm (6 in) longer than the curtain width.

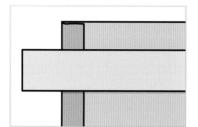

2 Open up the fold and place the buckram along the pressed line. Make sure the bottom edge of the buckram is along the fold.

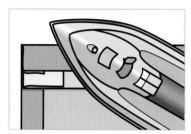

3 Fold in the extra buckram at each end, then fold over the extra fabric above the buckram. Press to hold in place.

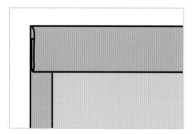

4 Fold over the buckram tape, so the line you first pressed is now back at the top of the curtain. Press across the width of the curtain again.

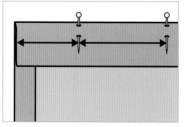

5 Measure and divide the curtain evenly into space, pleat, space across the top, with the pleat width a bit bigger than the space. For instance, if the space is 13 cm (5 in) the pleat should be around 19 cm (7.5 in). Place a pin at each measured point.

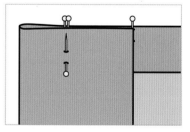

6 With the curtain face down, fold the first pin over to meet the second pin. Pin the pleat in place. Fold the third pin to meet the fourth and repeat across the curtain. On the right side, stitch down the pinned line of each pleat to the depth of the buckram.

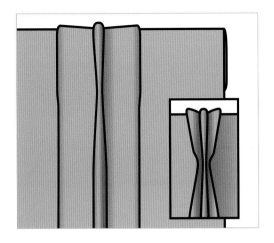

7 Still working from the right side, flatten each pleat slightly over the line of stitching. Pinch the centre up into a pleat, then pinch a pleat on each side. Adjust until you have three even pleats.

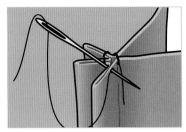

8 Work stab stitch through the base of each triple pleat to hold it firmly in position, pulling the thread tight and fastening off after each one. Close the top of each fold with slipstitch.

Goblet pleats

Goblet pleats are a relation of French pleats and make for an elegant, formal heading for lined and interlined curtains (see pages 44–49). However, they are quite heavy visually so this style needs to be used with care. The goblets are padded to create their solid, rounded shape. You will need two-and-a-half times the finished width and should add 20 cm (8 in) to the finished drop.

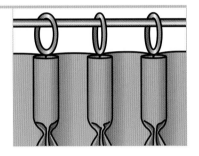

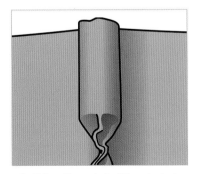

1 Follow Steps 1–6 of French pleats. Working on the right side, pinch together the base of the pleat and work a few stab stitches to hold it in place.

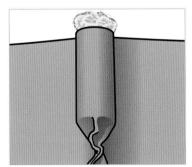

2 Pad out the rounded shape of each goblet with a roll of wadding or other soft material, pushing it right down to the bottom of the pleat.

Unlined curtains

These are the most basic style of curtain and are quick and easy to make. They do not provide warmth or darkness, just decoration and privacy. As there is no lining, the fabric will fade if the curtains are hung in a sunny window. If you have heavy interlined curtains in a room for the winter months, you can make light, unlined curtains to replace them for the summer. Changing curtains in this way really does give a room a fresh look for different seasons.

Fabric quantities

Choose a heading (see pages 32–41) and calculate the cut drop of the curtain (see pages 28–30). This curtain has a standard pencil pleat heading (see page 38).

Multiply the finished width of the curtain by the amount of fullness the heading requires.

Calculate the amount of fabric needed (see page 30).

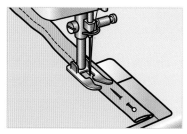

1 Join the widths of fabric needed to make the curtain (see page 91). On each side edge, turn under and stitch a double 2 cm (¾ in) hem.

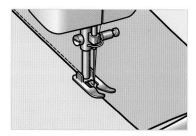

2 On the bottom edge, turn up 2 cm (¾ in) then 10 cm (4 in) to make a deep hem. Machine stitch it close to the upper edge.

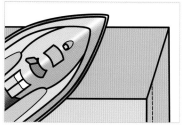

3 On the top edge, turn under the fabric to slightly less than the depth of the heading tape. Fold in the side edge at an angle, as shown, and press.

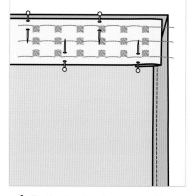

4 Pin the heading tape across the top of the curtain. The tape should cover the raw edge of the fabric and the top edge should be just below the top edge of the curtain. Pull the cords free.

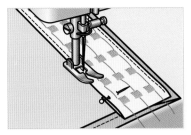

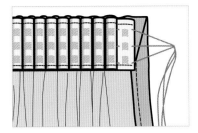

5 Stitch the heading tape in place across the top of the curtain. Be very careful not to catch the cords in the stitching.

6 Pull the cords to gather the tape up evenly until the curtain is the required width. Knot the cords securely and tuck the excess behind a group of cords in the heading tape.

Below: Lightweight fabric looks cool and pretty made up into simple unlined curtains to screen a kitchen instead of a wooden door.

Lined and interlined curtains

A traditional curtain has both lining and interlining, which are all attached so they move with the main fabric as one unit. This means that the completed curtain will hang beautifully. Three layers does make for quite a substantial curtain, so if you need something lighter then just omit the interlining layer.

Fabric quantities

Choose a heading (see pages 32–41) and calculate the cut drop of the curtain (see pages 28–30). This curtain has a pencil pleat heading (see page 38).

Multiply the finished width of the curtain by the amount of fullness the heading requires.

Calculate the amount of main fabric needed (see page 30).

The joined widths of lining should be the same length as but 10 cm (4 in) narrower than the joined widths of main fabric.

The joined widths of interlining should be as wide as the joined widths of main fabric, but 10 cm (4 in) shorter.

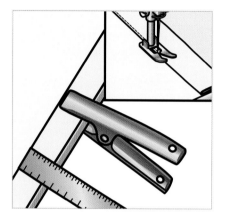

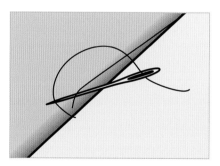

1 Join widths to make up the lining. Turn up a double 3 cm (1¼ in) hem along the bottom edge and press it. Stitch the hem close to the upper edge. Join the widths of interlining using a lapped seam (see page 92).

2 Lay the interlining out flat. Lay the main fabric flat on top of it with the top edge 8 cm (3 in) above the top edge of the interlining. Fold the main fabric back on itself in a straight line down the centre of the curtain. Work interlocking stitches (see page 93) 10 cm (4 in) apart to attach the two layers. Start and stop the stitching 20 cm (8 in) from the top and bottom edges of the fabric. Fold the main fabric flat again, then fold it back on itself again about 40 cm (16 in) away from and parallel to the line of interlocking stitches. Work another line of interlocking stitches. Repeat this across the curtain, making each line of stitches about 40 cm (16 in) apart. Carefully turn over the entire curtain, so the interlining is now on top.

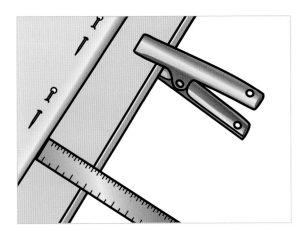

3 Fold the interlining back by 5 cm (2 in) along the length of the leading edge of the curtain. Measure at regular intervals to make sure the line stays straight. Pin the interlining in position.

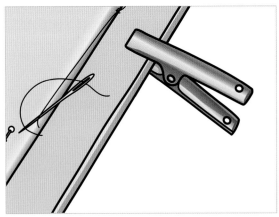

4 Work interlocking stitch along the fold you have just made, making the stitches about 5 cm (2 in) apart. This will secure the leading edge, which is handled more than other parts of the curtain.

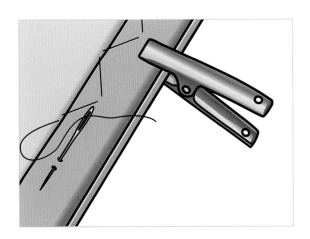

5 Fold the edge of the main curtain fabric over the interlining and anchor it in place with pyramid stitches (see page 93) making sure that the stitching does not show on the right side of the curtain. Repeat Steps 3–5 on the other side of the curtain.

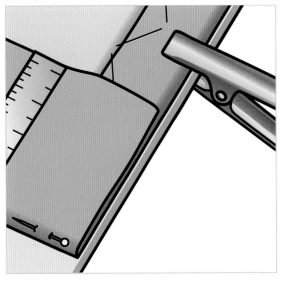

6 Along the bottom edge of the curtain, fold the main fabric up by 12 cm (5 in) over the interlining. Pin in position close to the fold.

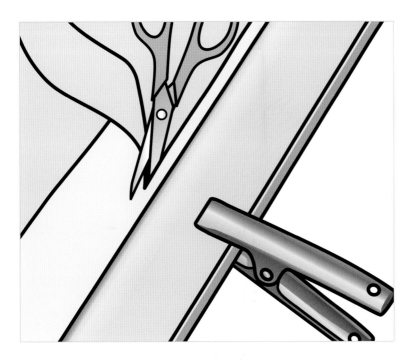

7 Turn the hem you just made back on itself: you will find it easiest to hold it back with a clamp or a few pins. Trim off 3 cm (1 ¼ in) of excess interlining, straightening up the edge as you go if necessary.

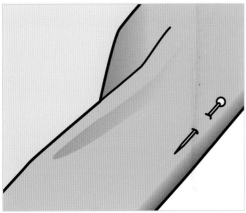

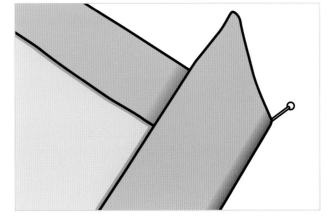

8 Release the edge of the hem and fold under the raw edge by 3 cm (1 ¼ in), holding it in place by moving up the pins from the fold line. The upper edge of the hem should cover the raw edge of the interlining. Leave the last 30 cm (12 in) unpinned at both ends of the hem.

9 Lay each end of the hem on a flat surface and check that the corner is a perfect right angle, gently smoothing out any wrinkles with your fingers. Stick a pin into the corner to mark it, then open out the hem section of the corner.

Left: Lined curtains are great in a bedroom as they not only keep the room cosy but also block out light.

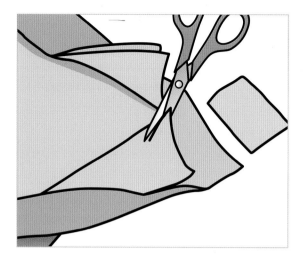

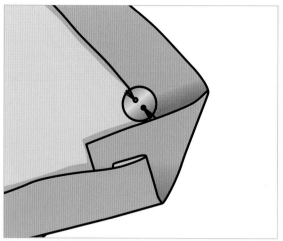

10 Open the hem and side seam out flat, making sure you can see the point of the pin that is marking the corner. Cut the interlining straight across from the side edge to the pin, then straight down to the bottom edge to remove a rectangle of interlining. Then cut from the pin at a 45° angle down to the hem to remove a triangle of interlining. This process removes the right shape of excess bulky interlining so that the corner will fold neatly.

11 Using double thread, stitch a curtain weight into each corner. Fold the main fabric side seam and hem back over the interlining, making a neat mitre at the corner, and slipstitch the hem in place.

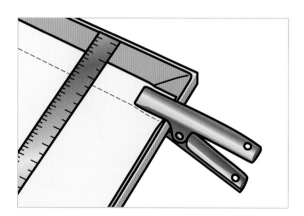

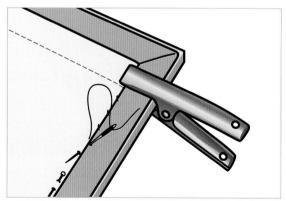

12 Place the lining on top of the curtain, right side up. Align the raw edge with the leading edge of the curtain at one side, but leave 3 cm (1¼ in) of the main fabric hem showing at the bottom. Clamp or pin in place.

13 Fold under the raw side edge of the lining by 3 cm (1¼ in), aligning the bottom corner with the corner fold of the main fabric. Slipstitch the lining to the main fabric along the leading edge, stopping about 20 cm (8 in) from the top of the curtain.

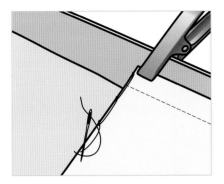

14 Fold the lining back on itself about 40 cm (16 in) from the edge and work interlocking stitch down the fold. Repeat across the curtain as in Step 2. On the far side, trim off any excess lining fabric then repeat Steps 12 and 13 on that side.

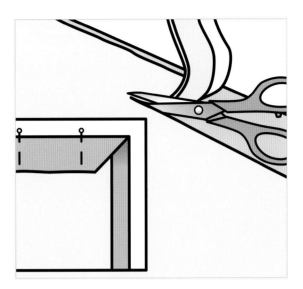

15 Measure the finished drop of the curtain up from the main hem and mark this distance across the heading of the curtain on the wrong side. Trim off the excess lining and interlining to this line, but DO NOT trim off the main fabric. Fold over the main fabric along the cut edge of the lining and interlining, turning the corner under at a 45° angle (see inset). Pin along the fold.

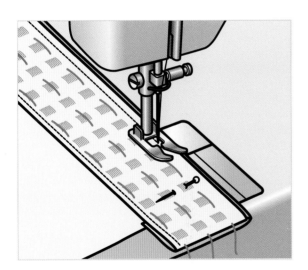

16 Pin the heading tape across the top of the curtain. The tape should cover the raw edge of the fabric and the top edge should be just below the top edge of the curtain. Pull the cords free. Stitch the heading tape in place across the top of the curtain. Be very careful not to catch the cords in the lines of stitching.

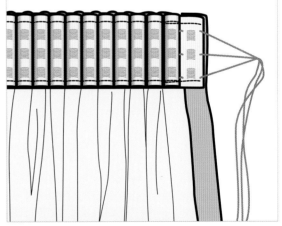

17 Pull the cords to gather the tape up evenly until the curtain heading is the required width. Knot the cords securely and tuck the excess behind a group of cords in the heading tape.

Tube lining

This method involves machine stitching the lining to the main fabric at each side, right sides together. The resulting tube is then turned right sides out for the hem and heading to be added. This is much faster than hand stitching the side seams, but means that the curtain cannot be interlined. However, if you want a lighter-weight curtain, this technique may be ideal.

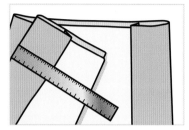

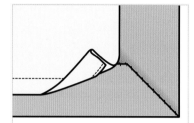

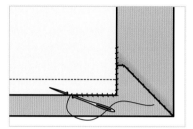

1 With right sides together and taking a 1.5 cm (⅝ in) seam, stitch the curtain to the lining on each side, starting and stopping 20 cm (8 in) from the top and bottom. Turn right sides out and measure each side so the lining is centred on the curtain, then press.

2 Turn up the bottom hem on the main fabric, and pin in place. Turn up a double hem on the lining so it is 4 cm (1½ in) shorter than the main fabric. Machine stitch the lining hem. Mitre the corners of the main fabric hem and slipstitch it in place.

3 Slipstitch the unattached ends of the sides of the lining to the main fabric. Turn the corner and continue stitching for a short distance, slipstitching the lining to the main fabric hem. Follow Steps 15–17 of Lined and Interlined Curtain (see pages 44–49) to make the heading.

Fabric quantities

Choose a heading (see pages 32–41) and calculate the cut drop of the curtain (see pages 28–30).

Multiply the finished width of the curtain by the amount of fullness the heading requires.

Calculate the amount of main fabric needed (see page 30).

The joined widths of lining should be the same length as but 20 cm (8 in) narrower than the joined widths of main fabric.

Loose linings

Here the lining is made as a totally separate piece to the curtain itself and just hooked onto the back of it, which is very useful if the lining needs to be laundered separately for any reason. It is also a good technique to use if you want to add linings to purchased ready-made curtains. Again, with this technique it is not possible to have interlining.

Fabric quantities

Cut widths of lining material to the same length as the completed curtain.

Join the widths until the lining is as wide as the completed curtain.

Flat loose linings

If you cannot release the heading of a ready-made curtain, or are worried that the hooked-on lining will add too much bulk to a heading once it is pulled up, you can make a flat lining. Follow the same procedure, but cut the lining only as wide as the curtain heading. Just hook the lining onto the back of the pulled-up curtain heading.

Left: If you want coloured linings for curtains you can use another fabric instead of lining material. Make sure the lining can be laundered the same way as the main fabric and be aware that the coloured lining may fade in the sun.

1 Turn under a double hem along both side edges of the lining, adjusting the hem depth so that the lining is narrower than the curtain on each side by just a little less than the depth of the curtain side hems. (If you laid the curtain face down and the lining face up on top of it, the outer edges of the lining would just overlap the inner edges of the curtain side hems.) Machine stitch the lining side hems.

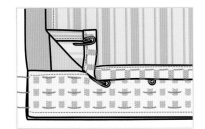

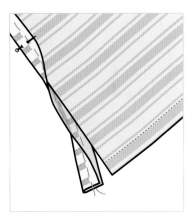

2 Pin a length of loose lining tape to enclose the raw edge of the top of the lining. Machine stitch the tape in position, making sure you stitch through all layers.

3 Insert hooks into the tape on the lining and then hook the lining to the back of the main curtain, using the bottom row of slots in the curtain heading tape. The lining can now be hemmed to a suitable length so it does not show below the curtain. Once the lining is hemmed, pull up the heading tape until the curtain is the right width.

Sheer curtains

Since these curtains are translucent, a basic construction method works best so that not too many seams show through. If you want a gathered heading you can buy translucent heading tape to use on this type of curtain, which will be much less obtrusive than the solid kind.

Fabric quantities

Measure the finished drop of the curtain and add 5 cm (2 in) for the hem.

Choose a heading (see pages 32–41) and calculate the cut drop of the curtain (see pages 28–30). This curtain has a casing heading (see page 34).

Multiply the finished width of the curtain by the amount of fullness the heading requires. If you can have whole numbers (two or three times width) then you do not have to hem the side seams.

Calculate the amount of fabric needed (see page 30).

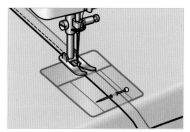

1 Do not cut the selvedges off the fabric. Overlapping them by the smallest amount possible and using a lapped seam (see page 92), join the fabric widths. If you have not been able to use selvedges as the side edges, then make very narrow double hems along those edges.

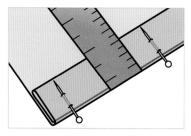

2 Turn up a double 2.5 cm (1 in) hem along the bottom edge and pin. Machine stitch very close to the upper folded edge.

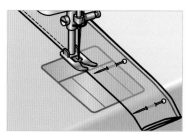

3 Fold and stitch the heading in the same way as the hem, but folding half the heading depth each time.

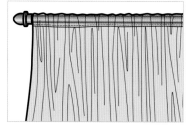

4 Carefully insert the rod into the casing you have made at the top, trying not to snag anywhere as threads will pull easily. Even out the gathers across the width of the curtain.

Right: Simple sheers obscure an unattractive view and offer privacy, but still let in lots of natural light.

Café curtains

Traditional café curtains have a scalloped or crenellated heading through which the pole or rod is threaded. They have no fullness and so hang completely flat across the lower half of the window. They offer some privacy but at the same time let in lots of natural light.

Fabric quantities

Measure the finished drop of the curtain and add 5 cm (2 in) for the hem.

Decide on the depth of the scallop you want and add twice this depth plus 6 cm (2½ in) to achieve the cut drop.

Divide the finished width of the curtain by the cut width of the fabric.

Calculate the amount of fabric needed (see page 30).

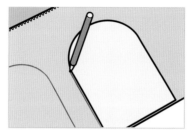

1 Make a paper template that is twice the depth of the final scallop shape you want. Adjust the width so that the shape will repeat evenly across the curtain. Join widths of fabric as required, then zigzag the raw edges at the top. Fold over the top edge to the right side to a level 6 cm (2½ in) deeper than the scallop template and pin. Mark out the scallops across the curtain width.

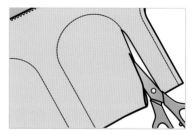

2 Pin around the edge of the middle section of each scallop, then stitch each scallop around the marked line. Using fabric shears, cut out the scallops and trim the fabric to within 1 cm (⅜ in) of the stitching line.

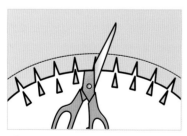

3 Clip tiny notches in the seam allowances around all curved parts of each scallop, being very careful not to cut through any of the stitching.

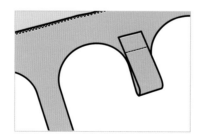

4 Turn the top of the curtain right side out – the edge you folded over has now become a facing along the top edge. Press gently, then fold each tab to the back so that the square end is level with the bottom of the scallop. Machine stitch the tabs to the main curtain to make a channel across the top of the scallops. Turn under a narrow double hem along the sides and stitch in place.

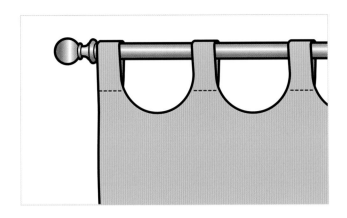

5 Thread the curtain onto the rod and check the position of the hem line. Trim off any excess fabric, then turn under and stitch a double 2.5 cm (1 in) hem along the bottom edge of the curtain.

Café curtain variations

There are different ways of attaching the curtains to the rod depending on the effect you want to achieve.

Tied heading

Here the curtain has been edged with a contrasting fabric and ties in the same fabric have been added to attach the curtain to the rod.

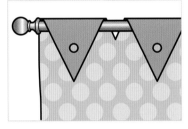

Triangles

These jaunty triangles have been made in the same way as the scallops, but are faced in a contrasting fabric and then folded to the front and secured with buttons.

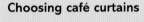

Choosing café curtains

This style of curtain was developed by – as the name suggests – cafés and restaurants. As they hang across only the bottom of a window the curtains gave the dining customer some privacy, but allow passers by to see into the restaurant. Café curtains are a good option for a living space that is mainly used during the day.

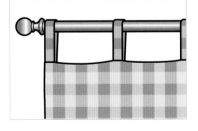

Tabbed heading

These narrow tabs can be made separately and inserted into the seam between the curtain and a facing. This allows you to use a matching or contrasting colour fabric.

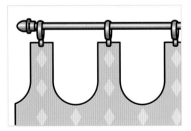

Scalloped with rings

Instead of folding over the tabs at the top, here the curtain is clipped to café curtain rings.

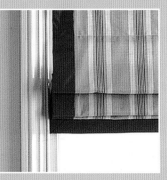

BLINDS

Measuring for blinds

Calculating fabric quantity

Roman blind

Soft pleat blind

Roller blind

Measuring for blinds

When they are pulled down blinds hang flat against the window, so any inaccuracies in measuring will be obvious. So do measure carefully using a metre (yard) rule or folding ruler and ask a friend to help if need be. Measuring terms are the same as for curtains (see page 28).

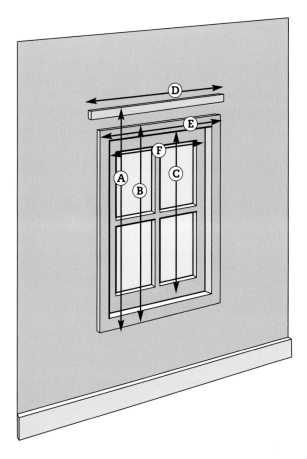

A Top of mounting board or track to bottom of window frame

B Top to bottom of window frame

C Top to bottom of window recess

D Length of mounting board or track

E Width of window frame from outside edge to outside edge

F Width of window recess

Blind fixtures

A Roman or soft pleat blind will hang from a mounting board that you make yourself (or you can buy a purpose-made track), while a roller blind has a purchased mechanism. A mounting board will usually be fixed to the wall above the window (D in the diagram) or across the width of the window frame (E in the diagram). If the latter, then bear in mind that when the blind is pulled up it will obscure the top of the window glass.

A roller blind is usually mounted across the width of the window frame (E in the diagram) or within the window recess (F in the diagram).

You need to attach a Roman or soft pleat blind to the mounting board before hanging the blind, but if you mark the position of it on the wall before you make up the blind then you'll have a fixed point to measure from.

Measure from the top of a mounting board to the required hem position. A roller blind kit will contain the necessary measuring instructions.

Blind width and length

If the blind is within the window recess or on the frame, then the width is dictated by those measurements. If it hangs from a mounting board on the wall, then the blind can be wider than the window frame, though more than 5 cm (2 in) wider on each side can look odd.

If the blind is within the recess, then the length of the recess determines the length of the blind. If the blind is on the frame or on the wall, then it can be longer than the window frame as long as there isn't a sill. However, blinds usually have a hem position at the bottom of the window frame. If you want the hem position to be below the frame, then make a light pencil mark on the wall at the required spot.

Taking measurements

As with measuring for curtains (see page 28) a metre (yard) rule or folding ruler is the ideal tool, but you can use a retractable metal tape measure.

To measure finished drop, hold your rule flat against the wall next to the window. Slide it up until the top is level with the top position of the blind (the top of the mounting board or top of the frame). If the window is tall then ask a friend to stand further back in the room and tell you when the top of the rule is in the right place. If you are measuring within the window recess, then place the rule against the inside edge of the frame and slide it up to the top of the recess.

If the blind hem position is within the length of the rule, then read off the measurement and make a note of it. If the blind will be longer than the rule, then make a light pencil mark on the wall at the bottom of the rule. Slide the rule down so that the top of it is against the pencil mark. Either read off the measurement at the position of the blind hem or repeat the process until you do reach the hem position. When you note the measurement, remember to add up all the lengths of rule that are marked on the wall as well as the final measurement.

If you are using a mounting board above the window, measure the length of that to establish the width of the blind. If the blind is on the frame or within the recess, then just measure that. When measuring a recess, take several width measurements at different heights and if they vary, work to the smallest one.

Joining fabric widths

If you do need to join widths for a blind, then avoid having a join down the centre of the blind where it will be very obvious. If you are joining two widths, cut one drop in half lengthways and match and stitch one half to either side of the uncut drop.

Calculating fabric quantity

Many blinds will need only a single width of fabric. However, if you do need to join widths, then allow for the pattern repeat as well as the hem and heading. The formulas given will help you work out how much fabric you need.

Cut drop for Roman blinds

To the finished drop measurement add the depth of your hem slat, plus 1 cm (⅜ in) ease, plus 2.5 cm (1 in).

Add an additional 8 cm (3 in) for fastening the blind to the mounting board.

If you are using patterned fabric, then check the pattern repeat and add one repeat. (You should do this even if you are not joining widths as the extra fabric will allow you to position the pattern on the blind to best advantage.)

This is your cut drop.

Cut drop for soft pleat blinds

To the finished drop measurement add 5 cm (2 in) for the hem.

Add an additional 8 cm (3 in) for fastening the blind to the mounting board.

If you are using patterned fabric, then check the pattern repeat and add one repeat. (You should do this even if you are not joining widths as the extra fabric will allow you to position the pattern on the blind to best advantage.)

This is your cut drop.

Amount of fabric to buy for Roman and soft pleat blinds

Add 6 cm (2½ in) to the finished width of the blind for side seams.

Divide the finished width by the cut width of your chosen fabric.

Round this up to the nearest half number (to allow for seams) to establish how many widths of fabric you will need.

Multiply the cut drop by the number of widths to calculate the required amount of fabric per blind.

Then round this up to the nearest sensible number.

An example for a Roman blind

Finished drop = 120 cm (48 in)
Add 9 cm (3½ in) for hem = 129 cm (51½ in)
Add 8 cm (3 in) for fastening = 137 cm (54½ in)
Add 35 cm (14 in) for pattern repeat = 172 cm (68½ in)
Cut drop is 172 cm (68½ in)

Width of window = 150 cm (60 in)
Side seams = 6 cm (2½ in)
Width needed for blind = 156 cm (62½ in)
Fabric width = 122 cm (48 in)
Divide 150 cm (60 in) by 122 (48) = 1.27 (1.30)
Round up to nearest half number = 1.5
Multiply 172 cm (68½ in) for cut drop by 1.5 = 258 cm (102¾ in)
Therefore the final amount of fabric = 258 cm (102¾ in), which is 2.58 m (2⅘ yd)
Round up to nearest sensible number = 275 cm (108 in), which is 2.75 m (3 yd)

Roller blinds

The kits for these do vary slightly so read the instructions carefully before you start the project. There will be instructions for measuring width and how much to add to the finished drop for hems and headings.

Left: Roman blinds can look beautiful made in sheer fabric, but the fabric will need to be stiffened or it won't pleat well.

Roman blind

A Roman blind looks very similar to a roller blind when it is pulled down, but it pulls up in a different way. When the cords at the side are pulled, strips of tape on the back of the blind pleat the fabric into neat horizontal folds at the top of the window. Roman blinds are ideal for windows that need a decorative dressing but that are not suitable for curtains.

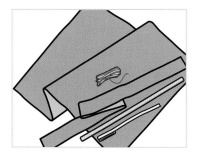

1 Cut and, if necessary join, the fabric for the blind. Cut a heading strip the width of the blind and 6 cm (2½ in) deep. You will also need several metres of Roman blind tape (or plain fabric tape and small curtain rings), thin cord, a wooden slat for the bottom and a mounting board (see Steps 6–10).

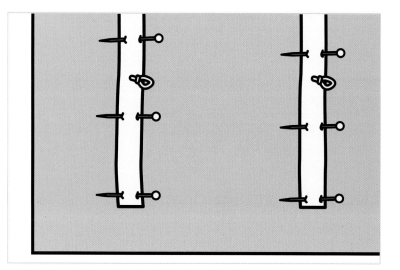

2 Mark guidelines on the wrong side of the blind for vertical tapes. One line should be about 7 cm (2¾ in) from each side edge, with other lines evenly spaced about 10 cm (4 in) apart across the full width of the blind. Starting the depth of the slat up from the bottom edge, pin the tape over the lines. Make sure that the first loop is more than the depth of the slat up from the start of the tape. It is vital that the loops on

each length of tape run in parallel horizontal lines across the blind or the pleats will not be even when the blind is pulled up. Machine stitch the tape in place along both long edges. Be careful not to catch the loops in the stitching. If you are using ordinary tape, stitch it on in the same way, then hand-stitch a small curtain ring at 10 cm (4 in) intervals up all the lengths of tape.

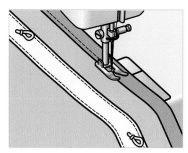

3 Turn under, pin and stitch a double 1.5 cm (⅝ in) hem along each side edge of the blind.

Right: A Roman blind will be appropriate for all sorts of rooms, depending on the fabric you choose. A geometric or plain fabric enhances the tailored look, while a floral or abstract pattern gives a softer effect.

Blinds

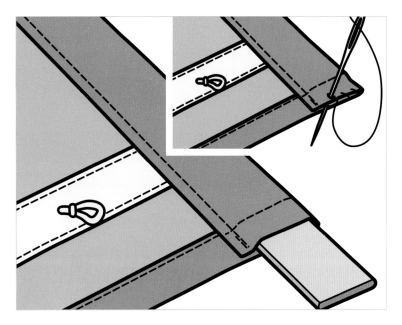

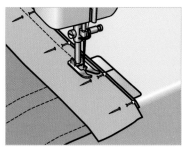

5 Right sides together, pin the heading strip across the top of the blind. Taking a 1.5 cm (⅝ in) seam allowance, stitch it in place. Fold under 1.5 cm (⅝ in) along the free edge of the strip, then fold the whole strip over the raw top edge of the blind to bind and strengthen it. Top stitch the binding in place on the wrong side.

4 Turn up the bottom edge by the depth of the slat plus 3 cm (1¼ in). Turn under 2 cm (¾ in) along the raw edge and pin. Machine stitch 5 mm (¼ in) from the fold to make a casing for the slat. Slide in the slat and slipstitch the ends of the casing closed.

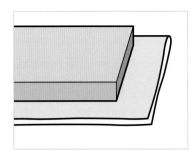

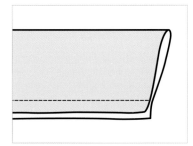

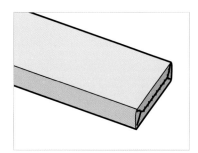

6 For the mounting board, cut a length of 2.5 x 5 cm (1 x 2 in) timber the finished width of the blind. Measure the width all around the board and cut a length of lining fabric to that size, plus 0.5 cm (¼ in) ease and 3 cm (1¼ in) seam allowance. The length of fabric required is the length of the cut board, plus 5 cm (2 in) at each end.

7 Right sides facing, fold the fabric in half lengthwise and, taking 1.5 cm (⅝ in) seam allowances, stitch the long edges together. Turn right side out.

8 Slide the board into the fabric tube. Fold the excess fabric at each end into a neat mitre and slipstitch in place to secure.

64

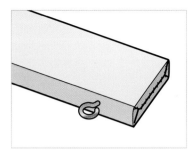

9 On one narrow edge of the mounting board, screw in an eye to align with each vertical length of tape.

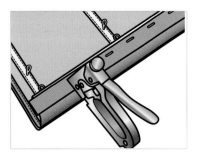

10 Using a staple gun or tacks, fix the wrong side of the top, bound edge of the blind to the side of the mounting board that will rest against the wall. Wrap the blind over to hang down the front of the board.

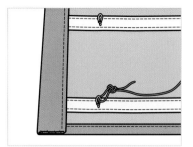

11 Slip the end of a length of cord through the bottom loop or curtain ring on one of the vertical tapes. Secure the cord with a strong knot at the end; it will need to be very firm as it will take the full weight every time the blind is pulled up.

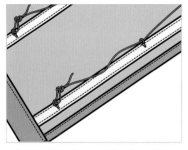

12 With the blind flat, thread the cord up through each loop in the tape, making sure that you leave enough cord at the top to stretch across the width of the blind. Repeat for each vertical tape across the blind.

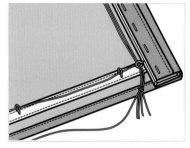

13 Thread the end of each cord through the screw eyes in one direction along the mounting board. Knot them together at the edge of the blind. Trim, then attach a separate length of cord to the knotted end to make a pull.

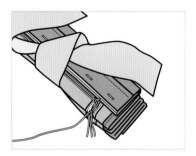

14 Fold the blind into even accordion pleats, aligning the tape loops, and tie it loosely with cotton tape at each end. Leave it tied up on a flat surface for a day or two to set the pleats into the fabric.

15 Screw through the mounting board directly into the window frame or wall, or mount the board on brackets. Mount a cleat hook on the wall on the pull cord side of the blind.

Soft pleat blind

These blinds are simple and unstructured, without tapes. Instead, rings are hand-stitched to the wrong side of the fabric in vertical lines, beginning 10 cm (4 in) from each side edge. To create even pleats, the rings must also run in horizontal parallel lines. The bottom ring should be 5 cm (2 in) from the hem, the highest 20 cm (8 in) from the top. The space in between the rings dictates the nature of the pleats that will form when the blind is pulled up.

Making up a basic soft pleat blind

Other than the tapes, the method for making a soft pleat blind is the same as for a Roman blind (see pages 62–65).
Cut and, if necessary join, the fabric for the blind. Cut a heading strip the width of the blind and 6 cm (2½ in) deep.

Turn under, pin and stitch a double 1.5 cm (⅝ in) hem along each side edge of the blind.

Turn under and stitch a double 2.5 cm (1 in) hem across the bottom edge.

Follow Steps 5–13 of Roman Blind to bind the top edge, attach it to the mounting board and cord up the blind.

Do not set the folds in the fabric, but just attach the mounting board to the window frame or wall.

Soft pleat blind with rod

This blind has one rod positioned about 15 cm (6 in) above the hem to give it weight. Sew on two rows of rings, with the bottom one 15 cm (6 in) above the rod and the others spaced the same distance apart. When pulled up this blind will look like a softer version of a Roman blind.

Full pleat blind

This blind is looser and fuller when it is pulled up. It has a row of rings up each side, 10 cm (4 in) from the edge, with the bottom ring 5 cm (2 in) from the base, the highest one 45 cm (18 in) from the top, and intervals of around 30 cm (12 in) between.

Ruched blind

The spacing of the rings on this blind is the same as the simpler full pleat blind shown left. However, the extra vertical lines of rings will produce a ruched effect when the blind is pulled up.

Making rod or slat casings

There are two ways of making casings to hold either rods or flat slats for the bottom of a soft pleat blind.

Slat casing

A flat slat sits better in this style of casing. Though the lines of stitching will show on the right side, the pattern on a fabric won't be interrupted.

You need strips of lightweight tape or fabric to make the casings. If you use tape then make sure it is about 1 cm (⅜ in) wider than the slat. If you use fabric, then cut the strips wider still and press under a narrow single hem on each edge.

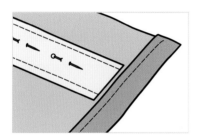

1 Make the side hems on the blind. Pin the tape to the back of the blind where you want the slat to be. Stitch along the long sides of the tape, as close to the edges as possible.

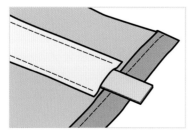

2 Slide the slat onto the casing and slipstitch the ends closed.

Rod casing

If the fabric is plain, then this is a quick and simple way of making a casing for a rod. However, if the fabric is patterned, then the pattern will be interrupted by the tuck in the fabric.

You need to add a casing allowance of the circumference of the rod plus 5 mm (¼ in) ease to the cut drop of the blind.

Below: Simple soft pleat blinds work well in very lightweight fabrics and offer a contemporary alternative to net curtains.

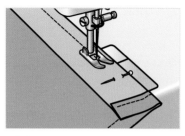

1 Make the side seams on the blind. Right sides facing, fold the fabric where you want the rod to be. Measure half the casing allowance from the fold and stitch a line right across the blind at this point. Slide the rod into the casing and slipstitch the ends closed.

Roller blind

Roller blinds are simple panels of fabric that roll onto a spring-loaded cylinder at the top of the blind. These blinds are often made of stiffened fabric, but there are kits available that mean you can use your own fabric to match the rest of an interior scheme.

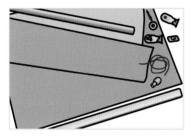

1 Measure, mark and cut a length of fabric following the manufacturer's instructions in the kit. Make sure the kit has all its parts, including a spring roller, a slat for the bottom, cord and small pieces of hardware.

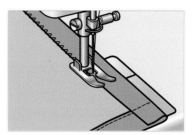

2 Turn under, pin and stitch a narrow hem on both sides of the length of fabric. Zigzag a single hem along the raw edge at the top.

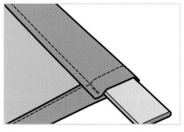

3 Turn up, pin and stitch the bottom edge to make a casing wide enough for the bottom slat. Insert the slat and slipstitch the end of the casing closed to hold it in place.

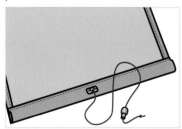

4 Attach the pull cord mechanism to the centre of the back of the slat. Thread the finial onto the cord and knot the end. Spray the blind with a coat of protective stiffener, if desired.

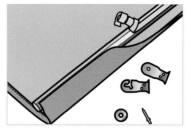

5 Attach the top edge of the fabric to the spring roller. The type illustrated has a self-adhesive strip onto which the fabric can be pressed. Some kits may have fixings that use staples or small tacks instead.

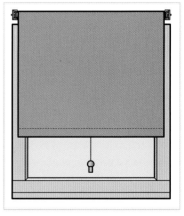

6 Mount the brackets on the window frame, wall or ceiling following the manufacturer's instructions. Roll the blind up and insert the end prongs into the brackets; pulling the blind up sets the mechanism.

Roller blind variations

Although roller blinds are simple in concept, they do not have to be plain or boring. The bottom edge can be finished with almost any type of trim, or it can be shaped.

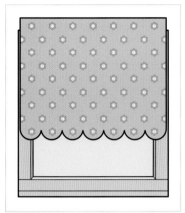

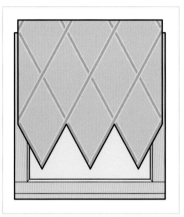

Scalloped edge

The scalloped edge of this blind was made and faced like the café curtains (see pages 54–55). The casing for the bottom slat is made like a slat casing for a soft pleat blind (see page 67).

Pointed edge

Here the pattern of the fabric has been used to create an effective and dramatic edging. The edges could be faced, turned back in a narrow hem or bound.

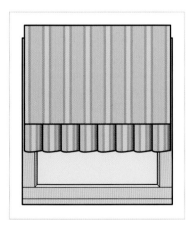

Pleated edge

The bottom trim of this blind is a separate strip of fabric that has been box-pleated and stitched to the bottom of the casing to make a stylish edge.

Right: Pretty patterned fabric can make a straightforward roller blind into a decorative window treatment.

FINISHING TOUCHES

Trims and embellishments

Attaching trims

Tiebacks and holdbacks

Making tiebacks

Trims and embellishments

Trims, tassels and buttons are a great way to add interest and detail to home furnishing projects, or to customize bought items easily. There is a wide range available: solid or multicoloured, textured or smooth, wide or narrow, elaborate or simple. Choosing the right one for your project is largely a matter of personal taste. Here are a few samples of some types of trim with advice on stitching them to your project by hand or with a sewing machine.

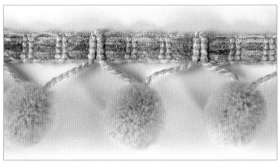

Bobble fringe

A fun fringe, these bobbles have a retro 1950s feel. A narrow, heavily textured header like this one would be tricky to stitch on neatly by machine; better to do it by hand.

Braid with tassels

Tassels are more three-dimensional than fringing, and are easy to add to any project with this tassel braid. Braids or fringes with a flat header, like this one, can be stitched to a project by hand or by sewing machine. Match the thread carefully and stitch through the header, close to the upper and lower edges.

Above: There are myriad different types of fringe of various weights, lengths, colours and fibres. Some have a decorative top edge (also called the header) or inset tassels or pom-poms, providing extra embellishment for no extra effort.

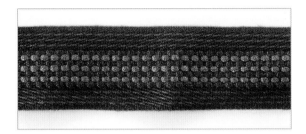

Deep border

A deep border is suitable for larger projects where narrow trims would be lost in scale. Stitch it to the project with a sewing machine, stitching close to one edge along the length of the border. Then go back to the end you started from and stitch the other edge. If you stitch in different directions along each edge, the border may twist slightly and won't lie flat.

Rope border

The colours in this simple rope border are toning shades so the effect is very subtle. Rope must be stitched on to a project by hand (see page 74).

Gimp braid

Gimp braid can add extra weight to lighter fabrics. You may be able to stitch it on with a machine, making a single line of stitching down the middle. However, most gimps are too thick for this and are best stitched on by hand.

Heavy fringe

This is a traditional fringe used for curtains, upholstery and tablecloths. If the header is quite flat, then it can be stitched to the back of the project, so that just the fringe peeps out from the edge (see page 74).

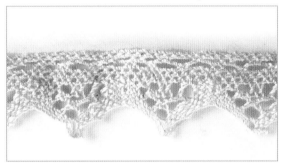

Antique lace

Delicate lace makes a great border for natural fabrics such as fine linen and cotton lawn. It also looks good with sheer fabrics. Stitch it on by hand or with a machine, whatever works best with the lace pattern you choose.

Attaching trims

You can attach trims to your project either by hand-stitching or with a sewing machine. The method you use will depend on the style of the trim. Always pick a thread colour that matches the trim as closely as possible, unless you are stitching the flat header of a trim to the back of the project, in which case the stitching will show on the front of the fabric and you need to match the thread to the fabric colour.

Hand-stitching rope border

Make firm hand stitches through and around the cut ends of the twisted rope to prevent it unravelling – which it can do remarkably quickly unless it is secured.

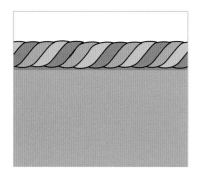

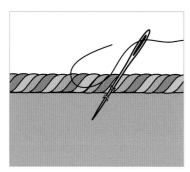

1 Make a tiny stitch through the rope, then a tiny stitch through the fabric. Pull the stitches tight and repeat along the length of the rope.

Machine-stitching fringe

This shows fringe stitched to the back of a project. The same principle applies if you are stitching it to the front.

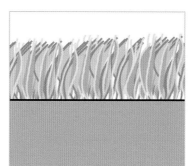

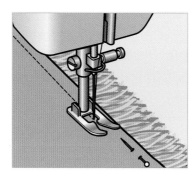

1 Pin, and if necessary tack, the fringe to the hemmed edge. Using thread that matches the fabric, machine stitch the fringe in position.

Measuring for trims

Remember that if you are going to add a fringe, bobble or tassel trim to the hem of a curtain or blind, you need to make the curtain or blind shorter by the depth of the trim. It's a good idea to stitch a short length of trim to a piece of fabric, using the technique you plan to use in the project. Check that you like the final effect, and measure how much the trim extends beyond the fabric. Subtract that measurement from the cut drop.

Right: This fine fringe complements the almost sheer fabric beautifully. You do need to consider the weight of a trim – both the physical and visual weight. A chunky trim can spoil the drape of a lightweight curtain and look odd, while a thin trim can be lost on a thick fabric.

Tiebacks and holdbacks

Tiebacks are lengths of fabric attached to a hook (or something similar) on the wall and are designed to hold the curtain back out of the way when it is pulled open. They also add an extra decorative touch. Holdbacks serve a similar purpose, but are made of a solid material, such as wood or metal, and are fixed to the wall so the curtain can be hooked behind them.

Single tassel tieback

These are available in all sorts of colours and sizes, so you should be able to find one to complement your curtain fabric. The ends of the cords have small rings attached to them that are slipped over a hook in the wall to hold the curtain back.

Double tassel tieback

A variation on the single tassel tieback, these will give a room a grander, more formal feel. You can pull the curtain fabric out a little above the tieback to create a fuller, more luxuriant look to the drawn curtains.

Plaited rope tieback

These can be bought or made to match a fabric. Pick thick furnishing rope in three colours or shades of a single colour. Hand-stitch the ends together, plait the rope to the required tieback length, cut and stitch the other ends. Bind the ends with thinner cord to neaten and sew on rings.

Above: Tiebacks can be very informal: a plain leather belt is the perfect foil to these thick wool check curtains.

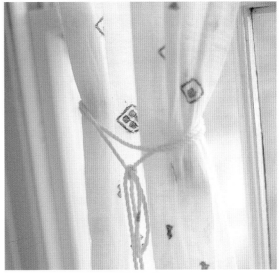

Above: If you are using tiebacks on sheer curtains, choose something visually light or the tieback will overwhelm the curtain.

Metal post holdback

These are made of polished brass, wrought iron, chrome or stainless steel. They are almost invariably round, with a short post at the back to hold them away from the wall and to provide a space for the curtain to sit within. They often have a decorative front that matches the finial of the curtain pole.

Metal hook holdback

These can be found in the same materials as metal post holdbacks. The large hook is fitted facing away from the curtain on each side, so the curtain can be slid into the open end of the hook and held back.

Cord tieback

A tieback doesn't have to be purpose-made: cord simply wrapped around the curtain can work very well in a casual room. Cords can also be twisted, plaited, knotted or just wound into a thick rope.

Making tiebacks

Fabric tiebacks can be made from the same fabric as the curtain, or in a co-ordinating colour. They can be trimmed to match the curtain, or other soft furnishings in a room.

Measuring for fabric tiebacks

To work out the best position for a tieback, hold the curtain back with a spare piece of fabric at different levels to see which one looks right. Traditionally, tiebacks sit about two-thirds of the height down from the top. Then pull the curtain back with the spare length of fabric until the curtain makes a nice rounded curve, not too tight or too loose. You can then measure the fabric piece to see how much you need for the tieback.

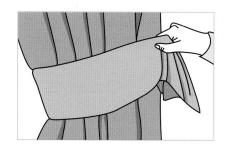

Basic tieback

Fabric tiebacks are usually a gentle crescent shape, but you can make yours more angular if that suits the style of the room. If you are unsure, make a practice tieback in scrap fabric to get the shape right.

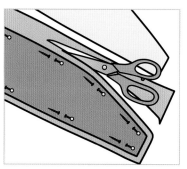

1 Make a paper template for your tieback. Cut out each tieback twice in fabric with seam allowances added, and once in iron-on interfacing.

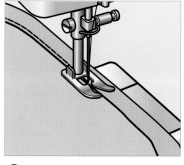

2 Place one piece of fabric wrong side up and iron the interfacing centrally on top. Place the other piece of fabric against the first, right sides together, and stitch all around the edge of the interfacing. Leave a gap to turn the tieback right side out.

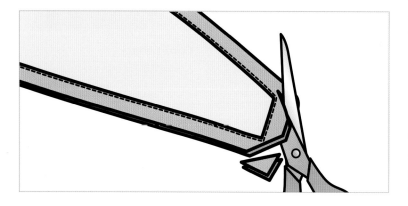

3 Notch the curves (see page 54) and clip off excess fabric across the corners. Turn the tieback right side out and slipstitch the gap closed. Press gently. Sew a metal ring to each end of the tieback.

Bound tieback

You can bind the edges of a basic tieback (see opposite), or bind a single piece of heavy fabric to make a simple tieback.

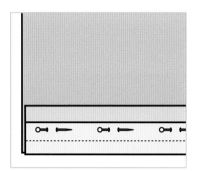

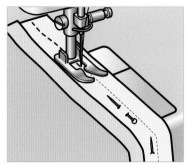

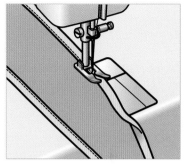

1 Open out one side of the binding and, right side down, pin it to the back of the fabric. Align the opened edge of the binding with the edge of the fabric. At the corners, mitre the binding neatly.

2 Machine stitch the binding in place right around the fabric, stitching along the fold in the opened-out side of the binding.

3 Fold the binding over to the right side of the fabric and pin in place. Adjust and fold the corners neatly. Top stitch right around the binding.

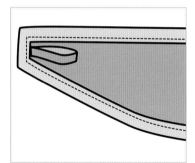

4 You can sew a ring to each end of the tieback, or incorporate fabric loops in the binding. To do this, hem a narrow strip of fabric. On the front of the tieback, tuck both ends of the strip under the edge of the binding and pin the loop in place. When you top stitch, make sure you catch the ends of the loop in the stitching.

Right: Thick cotton rope makes for a contemporary style of tieback. Bind the ends of the rope with jute string and make string loops to slip over wall hooks.

EQUIPMENT AND TECHNIQUES

Sewing equipment

Preparing and cutting fabric

Pattern matching

Sewing machines

Tension

Sewing machine stitches

Sewing an open seam

Sewing a lapped seam

Hand stitches

Sewing equipment

You don't need special equipment to make your own curtains and blinds, just the sewing basics. The only things you may not have that you'll find useful are a metre (yard) rule or folding rule for measuring your windows and clamps for holding large amounts of fabric.

Marking

There are all sorts of fabric markers on the market, but traditional chalk is probably the best type to use for marking out curtains.

◀ A chalk pencil has a chalk core instead of a lead one and often incorporates a brush at one end to easily remove marks once they are no longer needed.

▲ Tailor's chalk comes in a triangular shape that's easy to hold. It's available in white, blue and tan, so you can make a visible mark on any colour of fabric.

Measuring

You need a long rule for measuring windows and large lengths of fabric, and a small rule for hems and seams.

◀ A metre (yard) rule is the ideal piece of equipment for measuring windows (see page 29). A folding rule usually extends to 2 metres (yards) and so allows you to measure tall windows without a ladder.

▶ A set square is what's needed for marking and checking right angles.

▶ A retractable metal tape measure is a useful tool for measuring lengths of fabric. However, if you hold it up to measure a window it may buckle or twist and the measurements won't be accurate.

▶ A metal rule is what you need for measuring hem depths and seam allowance widths.

▶ A seam gauge can be useful, but certainly isn't essential. You set the red slider to the required hem/seam depth and then can quickly and accurately measure along a long edge.

Cutting

You'll need three pairs of scissors: one for cutting paper, one for cutting fabric and a small pair for snipping threads. Never cut paper with your fabric scissors as it really does blunt the blades.

▲ Fabric shears have blades angled to the handles. The blades slide along the surface without lifting the fabric much for more accurate cutting.

▲ Use small sewing scissors for clipping curves and corners and for snipping ends of thread.

▲ A seam ripper is a really useful tool for quickly and effectively cutting away threads if you have sewed a seam wrongly.

Holding

Pins will do most of the holding work, but clamps will be useful.

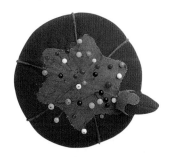

▲ Choose long pins with glass heads as you can see them easily and – unlike plastic heads – they won't melt if you catch them with the iron when pressing. Keep your pins in a pincushion, not a box.

Clamps can be bought in DIY shops as well as sewing shops: look for ones that aren't too tightly sprung or you'll struggle to open them. Also, do make sure they don't mark your table when you clamp fabric to it

Sewing

You'll need a sewing machine, but a basic model is perfectly suitable. It only needs straight stitch and zigzag stitch, nothing more fancy than that.

▲ The right-sized sewing machine needle for the fabric you are using is important. A 12/80 for lighter weight fabrics and a 14/90 for heavier ones will usually work well. If in doubt, ask advice in the shop you buy the fabric from.

A hand-sewing needle will be needed for some parts of projects; a standard sharps needle is a good all-rounder.

A long needle can be useful for tacking seams and hems

▲ The golden rule is to never buy cheap thread; it just tangles, knots and breaks and can spoil a project. Buy thread that is the same fibre as the fabric you are using, choosing a synthetic thread for wool fabrics. Match the colour as closely as possible to the fabric, going for thread that is a shade darker rather than lighter if there isn't a perfect match.

Preparing and cutting fabric

Accurate cutting is a must if you want your curtains to look professional. Start by making sure that the fabric is lying flat and is absolutely straight and square to the grain before you begin, and be careful not to stretch it out of shape as you work.

Preparing the fabric

Before you begin to cut, unroll the fabric and check along its entire length for any flaws in either the weave or the pattern. If there is a problem, the shop where you bought it should allow a return or exchange – but usually only if you have not started to cut. If the flaw is not serious you may be able to cut round it, but do not begin cutting until you are sure.

Fabrics that shrink should be washed and ironed before you cut into them. Follow the manufacturer's care guidelines for laundering.

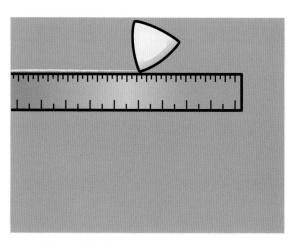

Marking fabric

Measure the finished drop you need and mark it at several points across the width of the fabric. Make sure the fabric stays flat and square while you are doing this. Lay a metal rule across the fabric, lining up all the marks, then lightly draw a chalk line against the edge of the rule. Use a set square to double-check that the line you have drawn is at right angles to the selvedge.

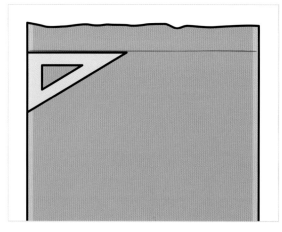

Straightening the fabric edge

Use a set square as illustrated to find the straight edge of the fabric at right angles to the selvedge. Check the weave; in some cases the fabric may have twisted during weaving. If so, pull out a thread across the width to establish the straight of grain, then pull the fabric gently in the opposite direction of the twist to straighten it.

Cutting sheers

To cut loosely-woven fabrics on the straight of grain, pull out a thread across the width and use the line created as your cutting line.

Cutting fabric

When cutting, turn the fabric around – or move yourself
around the fabric if that is easier – so that you are facing the
direction in which you want to cut. Always use sharp fabric
shears and try to keep the fabric as flat on the work surface
as possible while you make the cuts.

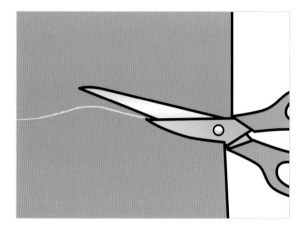

1 Open the blades of the shears as wide as is comfortable
and slide the lower blade under the fabric. Begin to close
the blades with a smooth action.

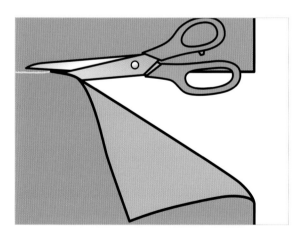

2 Do not completely close the blades or you will create a
jagged line. Instead, before the tips close, open the blades
up again, slide the lower blade further under the fabric and
repeat until you have completed the whole cut.

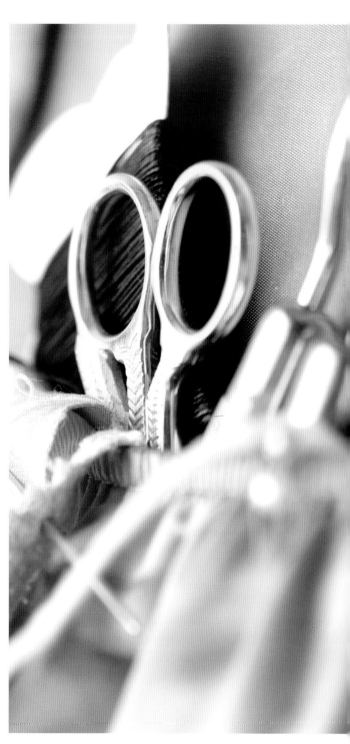

Pattern matching

If you want to join widths of patterned fabric it is important that you match the design across the seam as closely as possible. How well you do this really will make a difference to how good your finished curtains look.

Pattern repeats

In most patterned fabrics, whether they are woven or printed, the same motif or design will be repeated again and again down the length and across the width of the fabric. The distance between a recurring motif or section of design is the pattern repeat. The pattern repeat measurement should be given on the bolt of fabric. If not, you can measure it yourself.

Choose an easily identifiable part of the motif or design and measure from that point to the next identical point along the length of the fabric. Do this two or three times with different points to ensure that you have an accurate pattern repeat measurement.

When calculating fabric quantities for patterned fabrics, you need to add one pattern repeat to the finished drop (see page 30 and page 60).

Planning around the pattern repeat

The lengths of fabric needed for a curtain must be carefully planned to start and finish on the repeat in such a way that you can match the pattern across seams. This may mean that drops start at different places in the pattern, as shown below.

Mark the cutting line for each drop with chalk before starting to cut. Check that the pattern will match, then cut.

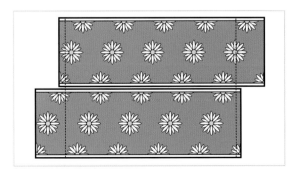

Cutting patterned fabric

With a large design, you may want to position motifs in a particular way on the finished curtain. Fold the fabric at different points in the design to see how the top and hem of the curtain will look before starting to cut.

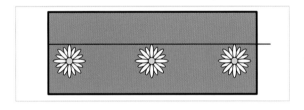

1 With a woven fabric, just make sure that the widthways threads are at a right angle to the selvedge. A good way to do this is to line up the selvedge with the side edge of a table, with the end of the fabric overhanging the table end. Crease the overhang along the table end to make a line across the pattern at right angles to the selvedge; then you can check the widthways threads against the crease line.

2 With a printed fabric the pattern may not run exactly along the straight of grain. With a small repeat this may not matter, but with large repeats it can be obvious. In this case you must cut to the pattern repeat and not to the true grain line, or your project will look wrong when it is finished. In this diagram the solid line is the straight of grain and the dotted line the line you need to cut to keep the pattern running true.

Matching the pattern

This is a quick and accurate way of matching a pattern
across a seam. Work carefully and pin and tack firmly
for the best result.

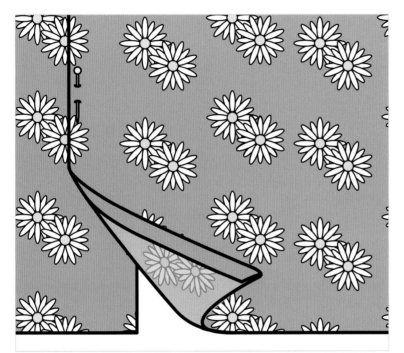

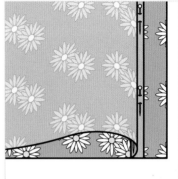

2 Fold the first piece of fabric
face down over the second piece,
exposing the trimmed edge that was
pressed under in Step 1. Carefully pin
this edge to the second piece of fabric.
Take out the pins on the right side.

1 Trim off the selvedge of one piece
to be joined and press 12 mm
(½ in) to the wrong side along the
trimmed edge. Lay the second piece of
fabric flat with right side up. Match the
pattern on the folded edge of the first
piece to the pattern on the second
piece. Pin in place very close to the
folded edge.

3 Stitch the seam from the wrong
side, stitching along the pressed
line. If you are worried about matching
the pattern, tack along this line first,
then open the fabric flat and check the
seam before machine stitching it.

4 Press the seam open. When you
look at the right side, the seam
(the solid line in this illustration) should
be almost invisible.

Sewing machines

The most expensive piece of equipment you will need to make your own curtains is a sewing machine. However, you won't need a top-of-the-range machine; straight stitch and zigzag stitch are the only stitches you'll use. But if you think you will do more sewing – maybe dressmaking – then it may well be worth investing in a machine with more functions.

Also bear in mind that very basic, inexpensive machines may not sew that well. You will usually be better off buying a mid-range machine from a good brand. Go to a sewing shop and try out the various machines, take advice from salespeople and from friends who are sewers before making your choice.

Your machine will have an instruction manual showing you how it works, but most machines have some common features.

Threading the top spool

Follow the instructions in the manual carefully; incorrect threading is a common cause of problems with a sewing machine. When threading the eye of the needle, make sure you pull the thread through far enough – 15 cm (6 in) is usually about right.

Threading the bobbin

Again, follow the manual carefully, making sure you have the bobbin the right way around in the case. Fit the case into the hook race unit. Turn the handwheel on the machine once to lower and raise the needle. The top spool thread will catch the bobbin thread and bring a loop of it up through the plate. Pull gently on the end of the top thread to pull the end of the bobbin thread through to the top.

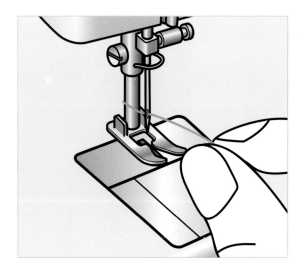

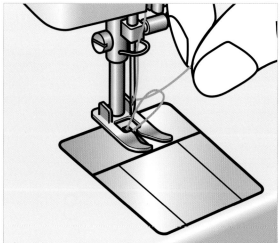

Tension

Both the top spool thread and the bobbin thread are held under tension by the machine. For perfect stitching the tension of both needs to be balanced. Many modern sewing machines have an automatic tension control, but older or more basic machines will need to have the tension adjusted manually. This is done by adjusting the top tension via a wheel on the front of the machine.

It is possible to adjust the bottom tension, usually by turning a screw in the bobbin case, but this should be a very last resort.

Even if your machine has an automatic tension control, you should always check the stitch tension by sewing on a scrap of the project fabric. Sew through as many layers as you will on the project; two layers for a seam, three for a double hem.

Balanced tension

If the tension is correct, the line of stitching will look exactly the same on both sides because the top spool thread (light blue) and the bobbin thread (dark blue) interlock within the layers of fabric. (You will almost invariably have the same coloured thread top and bottom; different colours are used here for clarity.)

Top spool thread too loose

In this instance the top thread has come all the way through the fabric and dots of it will show on the bobbin side. If you are unsure if this is happening, try sewing the test seam again with a contrast colour thread on the top spool so you can see the dots clearly.

Turn the tension wheel to one number higher to tighten the top spool tension, then sew another test seam to make sure the tension is now balanced.

Top spool thread too tight

Here the bobbin thread comes through to show on the top. You can check that this is the problem by sewing a test with a contrast bobbin thread.

Turn the tension wheel to one number lower to loosen the top spool tension, then sew another test seam.

Sewing machine stitches

You only need two machine stitches to make any of the projects in this book: straight stitch and zigzag stitch.

Straight stitch

This is the sewing machine stitch that you will use most often to stitch seams and hems.

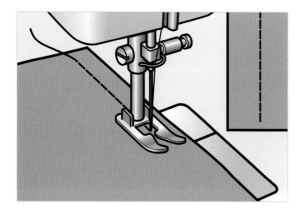

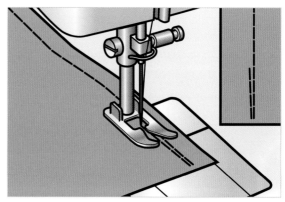

1 The project instructions will tell you what the seam allowance needs to be (this is how far from the edge of the fabric the line of stitching runs). A standard seam allowance is 1.5 cm (⅝ in). For most seams or hems in most fabrics the stitch length should be set to 3, but do sew a test seam on a scrap of fabric before starting a project.

2 To secure a line of stitching, sew a few reverse stitches at each end. Most sewing machines have this function: there will be a lever or button to hold down to make the machine sew in reverse. Start a seam about 1 cm (⅜ in) from the edge of the fabric, sew backwards to the edge, then sew the seam. At the end of the seam sew backwards for about 1 cm (⅜ in).

Zigzag stitch

This is primarily used along the raw edges of fabric to prevent them fraying.

1 The width and length of zigzag stitch can be adjusted to suit the fabric. Sew a test on a single layer of scrap fabric to ensure that the stitch does not pucker the fabric, creating a ridge in the seam allowance that can show as a bump on the right side when you press the seam open. For curtains, you can zigzag down the centre of the seam allowance and then trim any excess if the fabric is very thick.

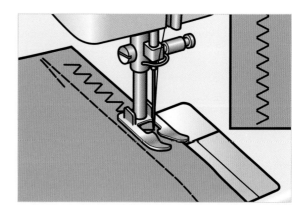

Sewing an open seam

A simple open seam is what is used to join widths of fabric for making curtains. If the fabric is patterned, then you will need to match the pattern across the seam (see pages 86–87).

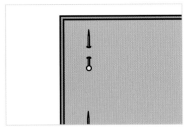

1 Right sides facing, pin together the pieces of fabric to be joined. Put the pins in with the points facing the end you will start sewing from: this way the heads are facing you as you sew the seam, making it easy to pull the pins out as you get to them.

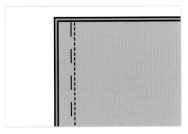

2 If necessary, tack the seam (this is a good idea if you are matching a pattern or if the fabric has a pile, such as velvet). Machine stitch the seam, reversing at each end to secure the line of stitching (see page 90).

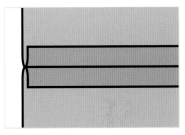

3 Take out any tacking threads and, if necessary trim the seam allowances.

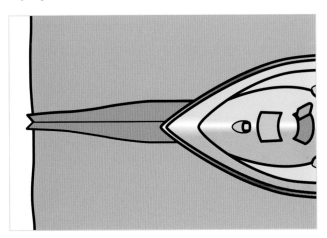

4 Press the seam allowances open. Remember to check any pressing information for the fabric first. If you are unsure of the fabric fibre content, press a scrap piece first to establish how hot the iron should be.

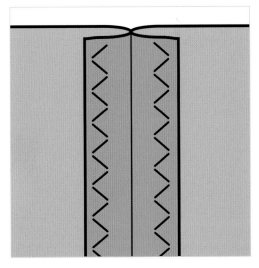

5 Zigzag along the edges of the seam allowances, stitching along the length of one seam allowance first, then the other one.

Sewing a lapped seam

This is used in curtain making to join widths of interlining (see page 44). It's also a good seam for joining the selvedge edges of widths of sheer fabric (see page 52).

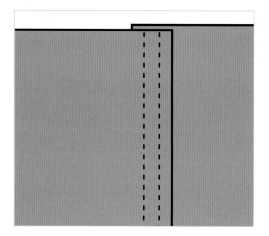

1 Simply lap the edges to be joined one over the other and pin together. For interlining the overlap should be 1 cm (⅜ in) and for sheer fabric, the depth of the selvedge. Sew a single or double (if the seam is likely to be pulled on) line of straight stitch along the overlapped section.

Pinning or tacking

Other than the scallops for café curtains (see pages 54–55), seams you sew for curtains and blinds are almost always straight. If the fabric doesn't have a pile or nap that may "creep" when sewing (see page 20), or isn't shiny and slippery, then pins should be enough to hold the seam while you machine stitch it. The only other occasion on which tacking may be a good idea is when you are matching patterns across a seam (see pages 86–87).

Hand stitches

There are some specialist hand stitches used in making curtains and blinds, but none are difficult to master.

Interlocking stitch

Use this stitch to attach the interlining to the main fabric (see page 44), and the lining to the interlining (see page 49).

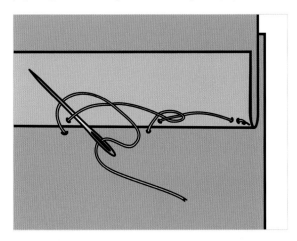

1 Knot the end of the thread and make a tiny stitch through the folded edge. Make a long stitch, taking the needle through the folded edge and making a tiny stitch through the layer of fabric underneath. When attaching the interlining to the main fabric, this tiny stitch must be invisible on the right side of the fabric. Do not pull the stitch tight or the fabric will pucker. Take the needle under the end of the last long stitch and over the thread going to the needle to lock the layers of fabric together at that point.

Pyramid stitch

This is the stitch used to hold the side edge of the curtain to the interlining (see page 45).

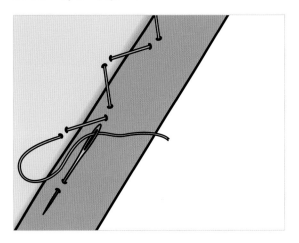

1 Knot the end of the thread and make a small stitch through the side edge. About 1.5 cm (⅝ in) further along, make a small stitch through the interlining. Moving along the same distance again, make a small stitch through the side edge. Continue in this way, zigzagging between the fabric and interlining, until the seam is completed.

Slipstitch

This stitch is mainly used to hem curtains or to attach the lining to the side edge (see page 48).

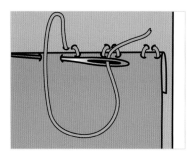

1 Bring the needle up through the folded edge of fabric. Make a tiny stitch through a couple of threads of the fabric just above the folded edge; the stitch should be invisible on the right side. Take the needle back down into the fold and slide it along a short distance before bringing it out again. Repeat along the hem.

Stab stitch

The base of French pleats (see page 40) and goblet pleats (see page 41) are stitched in this way. The stitch is shown here on French pleats.

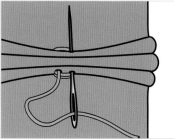

1 From the back, bring the needle through the fabric to one side of the pleats. Make a stitch straight through all the layers of pleats. A tiny distance away, make another stitch, parallel to the first one, back through the pleats. Make several stitches in this way, then secure the thread on the back.

Couching

This is the technique used to attach metal rings to the back of a soft pleat blind (see page 66). The same principle is used to hand-sew hooks for a curtain heading (see page 37).

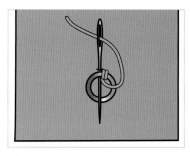

1 Make a series of small, tightly butted stitches through the main fabric and over the ring or hook. The number of stitches will depend on the size of the ring or hook and how much weight or strain it needs to take. On a soft pleat blind the stitches will show on the right side, so use a well-matched thread and make them as small as possible.

Glossary

bias strip or binding – a strip of fabric cut on a 45° angle to the straight grain of the fabric and used to bind edges, particularly curved ones. Bias-cut fabric stretches easily and so should ba handled with care. Bias binding can be made or bought commercially.

bolt – an amount of fabric wound on to a round cardboard tube or oval form. The fabric is usually folded lengthwise with the right sides together. The amount in a bolt depends on the type of fabric and the manufacturer.

casing – a hem, tuck or stitched-on strip into which a pole, rod or slat can be inserted.

drape – a fabric's ability to fall into folds: if it falls gracefully then it is said to drape well or have good drape.

ease – an amount added to a hem or seam allowance so that a fit is not too tight.

eyelet – two parts of a metal ring that are fitted together through a hole punched in the fabric.

feed dogs – the teeth under the throat plate of a sewing machine that feed the fabric through as it is stitched.

grain – the direction of the threads making up a woven fabric. There are two grains, the lengthwise (warp) grain and the widthwise or crosswise (weft) grain.

interfacing – a lightweight, stiff fabric that is used to give extra body to main fabric. Interfacing is available as sew-in and fusible – or iron-on – types. The latter is easy to use but is not suitable for all fabrics. Always test it on a scrap of project fabric.

interlining – a thick, soft, insulating fabric that can be inserted between the main fabric and lining of a curtain.

nap – also known as "pile". The projecting threads on the surface of a fabric such as velvet or corduroy.

notch – to make small, V-shaped cuts in the seam allowance of a curved seam so the seam is flat when turned right side out.

pattern repeat – the measurement between recurring motifs or sections of a design in a repeated pattern.

presser foot – the part of the sewing machine that holds the fabric against the feed dogs as it is being stitched.

raw edge – a cut edge of fabric that has not been finished off in any way.

seam allowance – the amount of fabric between the raw edge of the fabric and a line of stitching.

selvedge – the finished edge, formed during production, along either side of a length of fabric.

sheer – also referred to as "voile". Fabric that is semi-transparent. Curtains made from this fabric are known as "sheers" or "voiles".

straight of grain – threads running either parallel to or at right angles to the selvedge are on the straight of grain. The threads running at right angles (from selvedge to selvedge) are sometimes called "cross grain".

tacking – a line of stitching to temporarily hold layers of fabric together.

Index

Picture credits

ILLUSTRATIONS
Kang Chen, all pages except 74 by Barking Dog Art, and 86–87 by Stephen Dew

PHOTOGRAPHY
Tino Tedaldi:
2 top right and bottom right, 7, 13, 26 centre and right, 36, 43, 46, 53, 56 centre, 60, 67, 70 left and centre, 75, 77 top right

Lucinda Symons:
2 bottom left, 8 centre, 14, 17 top and bottom, 25, 35, 50, 56 left, 63, 70 right, 77 top left, 79

Michael Wicks:
18, 19, 59, 72 top and bottom right, 773, 80, 82, 83, 85, 92, 94

Michael Crockett: 72 left, 76, 77.

Holly Joliffe: 21, 26 left, 31

Debi Treloar: 8 right, 15

Colour in your home, Anova Books:
2 top left, 8 left, 22, 23

Louvolight: 56, 69

Every effort has been made to contact copyright holders. If you are aware of any unintentional omissions, please contact us directly so that any necessary corrections may be made for future editions.